E

E

Reflections on the Birth of the Elvis Faith

JOHN STRAUSBAUGH

BLAST BOOKS
New York

ISBN: 0-922233-15-2

Blast Books gratefully acknowledges the generous help of
Max Aguilera-Hellweg, Beth Escott, Zak Girdis,
Don Kennison, and Scott Lindgren

Photographs on pages 8, 38, 68, 84, 98, 116,
148, 170, 188, and 208 © 1994 Max Aguilera-Hellweg

Cover photograph and detail on title page © 1995 Scott Lindgren

Published by Blast Books, Inc.
P. O. Box 51
Cooper Station
New York, NY 10276-0051

Designed by Laura Lindgren

Manufactured in the United States of America
First Edition 1995

10 9 8 7 6 5 4 3 2 1

contents

acknowledgments

First, a disclaimer: My thanking individuals for their help does not imply that they agree with or support any of the opinions I express in this book. In fact, I'm quite sure a few of them will disagree with just about all of it.

So, thanks to:

Todd Morgan, communications director at Graceland; David Beckwith of The Beckwith Company, who handles press relations for Graceland; and all the Graceland staffers, for their assistance during Elvis Tribute Week 1994.

Darwin Lamm, founder and editor of *Elvis International Forum*, for research materials and personal insights.

Russ Smith, founder and editor of *NYPress*, where several portions of this book first appeared as articles.

Some friends and colleagues at *NYPress* who pointed me toward useful research materials, lent me books, and helped me think through some of my arguments. They include Godfrey Cheshire, who introduced me to the stunning resonances between Elvis and the Roman boy-god Antinous; Jim Knipfel, who clued me to some sources of Elvisology I might have overlooked; and Sam Sifton, who discussed many of my theories with me. And Paul Demko who, as an intern at *NYPress*, was a resourceful research assistant.

Carole Carroll, for Elvii info.

Ken Swezey and Laura Lindgren, publishers of Blast Books, for giving me the opportunity, encouragement, and resources to do this, my third book with them. Also Don Kennison, Max "T. C." Aguilera-Hellweg, and Beth Escott.

And Diane Ramo, with love, for sharing with me her knowledge of sacred ritual, helping me think through other ideas and opinions, and for putting up with me—and an awful lot of Elvis—during the making of this book.

L E T

T H E R E

B E   E L V I S

God was sitting, pondering the woes of the world one day, and he decided what the world needed was an emissary of beauty, form, and musical magic to bring joy to the troubled planet called Earth.

So God said, "Let there be a manchild made in Heaven, then put upon the earth . . . he will grow tall and straight and handsome; I will give him a loyal and loving heart filled with empathy and compassion; I will give him soulful eyes to warm many hearts; I will give him a majestic form and graceful poetic hands with which to express himself; then I will make his voice of crushed velvet, and when he speaks and sings, untold beauty and joy will be heard and felt throughout the world by all my children, by all the peoples of the world. I will bring him forth into the world to bring people together, and to give harmony to the lives of the multitudes; I will give him a vivacity and wit and personality that will warm and thrill all who witness this Heavenly Child; I will give him riches and love beyond imagination. . . . I will make him unique and irreplaceable, in a world of duplication; I will present him to the world . . . as a gift from God in Heaven . . . and he will be called . . .'ELVIS PRESLEY.'"

Anonymous

ELVIS IS A GOD. Not the One True God of a monotheism like Islam, Judaism, or Christianity, but a modern pagan god, one of the thousands whom people have worshipped throughout human existence, across many cultures. Like many before him, he was declared immortal when he died, and he is beginning to be worshipped as a divinity.

While millions upon millions of people are "Elvis fans," there's a hardcore of his most devoted followers who are something more than fans. It's a distinction they make themselves: they call themselves Elvis' "friends," to distinguish themselves from mere fans, and some of them call Elvis "E," the nickname used by his close friends while he was alive. The religiosity of this devoted hardcore has been noted for many years; Church of Elvis jokes were already in circulation before Elvis' death.

Are E's followers forming an indigenous American religious movement, like Mormonism or Black Islam? Right now it's still in its nascent, amorphous state, disorganized and dispersed, the way many religions begin. No prophet, no Paul or Brigham Young, has yet appeared to organize it. Like the very earliest Jesus cultists, the people I call Elvists are doing it themselves, intuitively and organically developing their own codes and rituals.

Elvism is often mocked and maligned as a kind of pseudo-religion, a particularly intense genre of celebrity worship with (blasphemous) religious overtones. But Elvis faith is in fact consistent with contemporary trends in American religious expression. That so many of these trends are outside established mainstream churches begs a redefinition of common assumptions about what constitutes religion, rather than a hasty slap of the *pseudo*- label on every new or unusual faith.

In the last quarter of the twentieth century there has been an explosion of religious and spiritual experimentation in America. Much of it has been characterized by a highly individualized, do-it-yourself approach that some have labeled "cafeteria religion"—personal, homemade belief systems that individuals create to suit their own tastes by picking and choosing from the smorgasbord of religions available to them. On the one hand, these include extremes within well-established traditions, such as the rise in fundamentalist, charismatic, and evangelical sects in Christianity, Islam, and Judaism. On the other, people are exploring an array of "alternative" and non-traditional belief systems, including everything that comes under the heading of "New Age" beliefs, variations on Eastern mysticism, spiritism and channeling, Wicca and Goddess worship, Magick and Satanism, Santeria, "neo-paganism," and techno-cults like Scientology and UFO religions.

Even in this earliest stage, several religious characteristics of Elvism are identifiable:

- E's followers pray to and through Elvis, a mythic king who's gone but not dead.
- They have a clear image of Elvis as a supernatural spiritual being who has ascended to heaven, where he watches over them and may intervene on their behalf.

- They claim that Elvis has effected miraculous cures and apparitions.
- Some of them have apocalyptic expectations that he will return to earth as a messiah in the near future. Others fully expect to join him on the heavenly spiritual plane.
- They make annual pilgrimages to Graceland and worship at his (possibly empty) tomb.
- They have created thousands of smaller shrines to him around the world.
- They revere sacred icons and relics associated with him.
- They observe the rudimentary outlines of a sacred calendar, with holy days and feast days.
- They are developing and beginning to codify a canon, liturgy, and scriptures.
- They testify and do good works in Elvis' name.
- In the "Elvii," the Elvis impersonators, they have the makings of a priestly caste, complete with vestments and rites.
- In the fan clubs, they have something that could turn into orders of nuns; in corporate Graceland, a potential Vatican.

Somewhere Elvis is smiling,
somewhere high in the sky.
Somewhere Elvis is singing his song,
and if you listen you could almost sing along.

Oh somewhere, somewhere in Heaven,
somewhere deep in the blue.
Angels are gathering to welcome home
a brand "New Star,"
and somewhere, Elvis is smiling at you.

JIMMY CRANE

One scholar of southern culture has called Elvism a "secular religion." Elvism is part of a larger move from *populist religions*, like Santeria or Mediterranean Catholicism, to *popular-culture religions*. The degree to which popular culture impinges on all facets of modern life and influences the formation of belief systems cannot be overstated. If Western civilization, with its mass media and all-pervasive transmission of commercial culture, "killed God" in the first half of the twentieth century, in the latter half of the century this same popular culture busied itself refilling the void it had created, providing the masses with new myths, new legends, a new pantheon of pop-star gods. Along with Elvis, some of the other figures who have been proposed, with varying degrees of plausibility, for inclusion in this pop-culture pantheon are JFK and Marilyn Monroe; John Lennon and Jim Morrison; "living saints" with undeniable cult followings, like the Grateful Dead; and the characters of *Star Trek*.

The tendency to worship and deify heroic figures is not new. On the contrary, it is clearly a fundamental human characteristic that has been the basis of much religion, myth creation, and even political practice throughout the ages.

If you can't take an Elvis religion seriously, maybe you're trying too hard. Maybe you're too rigid about religion in general. It may be helpful to think of Elvis religion—and many other cafeteria religions—as a *recreational religion*.[†] In contrast to established churchs' segregation of what Mircea Eliade calls the sacred and profane, recreational religions are more holistic, more integrated as a function of lifestyle: the infusion of religious fervor and faith into the pursuit of an avocation one intensely *enjoys*. In this sense, the practice of a recreational religion like

---

[†] A variant "recreational Christianity" was coined by "Brother Randall," editor and publisher of the Austin, Texas, fanzine *Snake Oil*. Brother Randall keeps tabs on many of the fringe and cult religions mentioned in this book, including Elvism.

Elvism can be compared to dedicated participation in a hobby, with ritual gatherings of hobbyists brought together by their shared avocation and their own language, codes of dress, and behavior, in which one acquires authority and/or seniority by mastering ascending levels of esoteric knowledge.

This meshing of faith and fun can certainly be confusing; we're more accustomed to a strict separation of the sacred and profane, of church and state. Can we speak of "devout" Trekkies or model-train enthusiasts? Certainly. Are they religious cults? Probably not. They are secular cults—though it has been argued that Trekkies are well on the way to transforming into a kind of pop-culture philosophical discipline, with a fairly well defined cosmology and code of behavior. Maybe Trekism is something like a late-twentieth-century American Confucianism to Elvism's late-twentieth-century Taoism.

Our century is by no means the first to witness an eruption of nontraditional and New Agey trends. In the second half of the 1800s there was an explosion of do-it-yourself religions and rogue sects throughout Europe, England, and America on a scale not seen since the Reformation. Establishment churches were experiencing a decline at that time, too, attacked by scientific atheists and freethinkers on one side and by newfangled spiritualists on the other. The latter were very much the precursors to the New Age phenomena of a century later: spirit-channeling (aka mediumistic séances), the anticipation of imminent apocalypse, interest in paganism and Eastern mysticism, feminism, vegetarianism, alternative sexuality, and alternative medicines all came into vogue between the late 1840s and 1900.

Meanwhile, nominally Christian sects led by charismatic preacher-gurus, some of whom concocted a spicy mix of spirituality and sexuality, attracted large followings of educated, middle-class believers, the core (but far from all) of them middle-aged women. Sociologists call them "coterie cults."

Rasputin's parlor-room cult in the Romanovs' St. Petersburg is cited as an example. The resonances with Elvism are clear.

■ ■ ■

I thought I'd had about all I could take,
With Elvis gone, all that was left was my hate.
I hated the world that had taken his all,
And left me with nothing but empty performance halls.

The hate grew worse, I was feeling the pain,
When I heard a voice say, "Hey man, let me explain.
Now don't feel sad for me, 'cause this was the plan,
I spent my time with you, now I'm with the MAN!

"My times with you were short—you had my love,
But now it's time for me, here up above.
I've loved you all, I hope there's no doubt,
I did my best, I sung my heart out.

. . . .

"You see, the MAN kinda liked my singin' too,
So he said: 'Come on Elvis, I have a choir for you!'

. . . .

"And my band? Man you should see it,
I've got old Gabriel playing first trumpet.
For back up? Well, I've got the most,
They call themselves The Heavenly Hosts!"

. . . .

With those last words, I slowly stood,
I knew life would go on, and knew that it should.
I felt much better, because from out of the blue,
Elvis had told me that he loved me too.

DAVID L. McCOY

The voice of an angel.
A man that reflects love, hope and desire.
A true expression of God.
Elvis.

CAROLYN FOX

"No Elvis lover I'm aware of would directly compare the King of the Jews to the King," Simon Hoggart once wrote in an article for *The Economist* entitled "Elvis of Nazareth." "But the reminders persist, and I suspect there is a good deal of picking and choosing, mainly subconscious, in making the Elvis myth. . . . For many Americans, the late Mr. Presley has become a religious figure, offering spiritual comfort which may not be so easily available in churches. . . . The Elvis myth was being formed while Elvis was still alive, and it's startling how often it jibes with the other great story American people, even—perhaps especially—near-illiterate southerners, learn at their mothers' knees."

That the Elvis faith has adopted Christian trappings is hardly surprising—Christianity is the dominant religious milieu in which Elvism has arisen, and it is the religious system Elvis followers know best.

When Elvists use words or images to depict Elvis in heaven, it is a distinctly Christian heaven ruled by the Christian God. (Interestingly, Jesus is almost never mentioned as being there with him.) When Elvists describe his humble birth in a Tupelo, Mississippi, shack, praise his devotion to his sainted mother Gladys, relate his miracles, defend him from his philistinic detractors, marvel at how he suffered and sacrificed for them, condemn the disciples who abandoned him, and say they're expecting his Second Coming—it is clear they are borrowing these notions.

This process of syncretism, the fusion of divergent beliefs, is common to many religious systems. Most of the world's major religions—those of the ancient Egyptians, Greeks, and

Romans, as well as Judaism, Christianity, and Islam—incorporated prior or concurrent religions. Many popular modern American faiths are syncretic, including Mormonism, Seventh Day Adventism, Santeria, the Unification Church, and Black Islam. Just as Jesus and his cult began as Jews, Elvis and his cult are starting out as Christians.

At the same time, Elvists are acutely sensitive to charges of blasphemy and sacrilege, and many years of mockery have made them understandably defensive about their faith. Many of the same people who openly confess they consider Elvis "the second-greatest man on earth since Jesus" (as one fan put it) and worship Elvis in any acceptable sense of that term also deny that they believe he's a god or that they as a group constitute a religion. Even among Elvis fans, those who openly express their veneration in religious terms can be treated with, at best, a chary tolerance. And even though Elvis himself was preoccupied for years with similarities between himself and Jesus, he issued pretty strict injunctions against his followers thinking of him as another Christ.

"The basic truth is that we made him a god, but he was only a man," says tv host Wink Martindale, who helped promote Elvis in his early years and remained on friendly terms with him. "We called him the King of Rock 'n' Roll, but his response to that was always the same. Thank you, but there is but one King: Jesus Christ."

"He detested it," his friend and backup singer J. D. Sumner agrees. "He loved to be just called a singer. . . . He never liked to be called the 'King.' In his mind, there was only one 'King' and that is Jesus Christ."

In the same breath, however, Sumner preaches a message awfully like an Elvist sermonette, neatly encapsulating some conflicts and contradictions inherent in the Elvis faith: "Remember this, next to the name of Jesus Christ, in all the history of the world, Elvis Presley's name is known second only to

Jesus. And he was still a regular human being, just like you and me. He was not a god. He never thought he was. He was very sincere, a humanitarian. If I've ever had a friend in this world, it was Elvis Presley. I have prayed with him, cried with him, and cussed with him. He was a great man and I loved him."

This kind of protesting-too-much is characteristic in many expressions of the Elvis faith. E was not *the* King, but he *was* second only to Jesus Christ. Much as Jesus made weak protestations of his humanity in the New Testament, Elvis' followers proclaim that he wasn't a saint, but he *was* the kindest, humblest, most generous and loving *man* who ever lived. . . .

Both Martindale and Sumner insist on portraying E as a God-fearing *Christian* man—though clearly a Christian man with a very special mission from God.

Sumner says, "Elvis was a religious man. He was one of the finest men that I have ever known and I believe that he was as much in God's grace as any man who has ever lived. . . . I've spent many a night talking about Jesus and the Bible with Elvis. I've prayed with him more than with anybody in my life. Sometimes I've wondered . . . about whether Elvis had a kind of ministry. He drew in thousands of people and witnessed to them in a way. . . ."

"God-fearing?" Martindale asks rhetorically. "Yes! For all of his 42 years. His humble beginning in that little Mississippi shack and the Christian upbringing by a devoted mother and father lighted a path that he would follow for the rest of his mortal life.

"Stray from that path? No question about it. For he was only human and humans make mistakes."

Among E's original Memphis Mafia, only George Klein, a disc jockey and longtime friend, seems unafraid of coming right out and saying it: "I don't mean to sound sacrilegious," he once told *Newsweek*, "but he was Jesus-like." "To hear people like Klein talk," *Reader's Digest* noted in a 1993 article, Elvis "all but walked on water. . . ."

Similarly, Elvis' faithful resist coming right out and calling Elvis a god, but they repeatedly tiptoe up to it. One fan describes his appearance on stage in Las Vegas as "this God-like Icon." Another fan writes, "In my eyes he was perfect, almost God-like." Pharmacist and Elvis impersonator Bert Hathaway declares, "Elvis, by far, is the greatest person who ever walked the face of the earth. No one, and I mean no one, will ever replace him."

Elvists who were raised Prostestant were taught to believe that praying to saints, the Virgin Mary, or anyone besides God the Father and Jesus Christ is papist blasphemy. Roman Catholics are considerably freer about who they may pray to. Over the centuries the Catholic Church has declared hundreds upon hundreds of mortals to be saints and has worked out a rigorous testing system for their canonization, complete with proofs, such as documented miracles and a series of hurdles the saint in the making must overcome on the way to sainthood. Catholicism, especially the old-fashioned variety predating the modernizing reforms of the Second Vatican Council in the 1960s, nurtured many avid cults of saints, the Virgin, and Joseph.

■　■　■

Skeptical outsiders often wonder how Elvis' followers can reconcile their apparent idolatry of him with whatever traditional religions they simultaneously practice. Down South, there's a saying that in every poor black home there are two pictures on the wall—Jesus and Martin Luther King, Jr. Poor white homes also have two: Jesus and Elvis. How can they worship Jesus *and* Elvis? Why doesn't that conflict with their Christian convictions?

Many parallels to the contradictions found in Elvis worship can be seen in folklorist Gillian Bennett's study of belief in the supernatural among middle-class British women. The majority of the women she studied believed in phenomena like ESP, premonitions, even contact with the dead. Contrary to stereotype, these weren't uneducated, lower-class drudges given to frequenting palm readers and devouring supermarket tabloids. They were educated middle-class suburban women, "pillars of the Church and local community, essentially 'respectable' in even the narrowest sense of that unpleasant term."

To discover how these women reconciled their conventional Church of England faith with their more outré "superstitious" beliefs, Bennett examined which superstitions they chose to accept and which they were prone to reject. She found that the supernatural beliefs they accepted were those that seemed to fit best with their understanding of their proper roles as middle-aged, middle-class women in British society.

"Popular beliefs reflect permitted behavior," Bennett concluded. "Like it or not, these women have been taught by the society they have grown up in that the ideal member of their sex is an intuitive, gentle, unassertive person, geared to a caring and supportive role. . . . Whether a particular traditional supernatural belief is acceptable seems to be directly governed by these basic assumptions."

These women tended to believe in phenomena like premonitions and telepathy because these sit well with the image of women as more intuitive and caring than males. They were far less likely to believe in palm reading or astrology, because these struck them as inappropriately self-centered pursuits. Similarly, they were more likely to believe in good spirits—the nurturing spiritual presence of a dead parent or late husband—than in bad spirits like poltergeists. The latter are "dangerous and unpredictable," Bennett writes, and "the women show a strong reluctance to believe in anything which makes the world seem unsafe."

The Elvis worshipped by his followers is a familiar spirit. And he is kind, loving, nurturing, sexy, generous, and consoling. "For Thelma Latronica, 69 years old, from Spokane, Wash., he was a replacement for a husband who died, a son she never knew," a 1987 *New York Times* report on Graceland pilgrims relates. "For some, like Betty Lou Watts of Severna Park, Md., who brought, among other things, an eight-foot-tall Elvis memorial for her motel room, Elvis is the one person she can turn to in the middle of the night. As she said, 'At three in the morning, you might need a special friend.'" Another fan told *Reader's Digest*, "When I was a teen-ager and something would go wrong in my life, I would go home and play Elvis records, and whatever felt bad inside would go away...."

"The love Elvis gave to the world can never be equalled by another person," one fan writes. "He was so wonderful and so giving, and we never gave him back all that we should have.... I feel that we should have loved him a little less and given him the freedom to live as we lived.... We just loved him to death and I feel so responsible for the part I might have played in this.... I know he loved us in spite of it, because that's the kind of man he was. He was always a giver and never a taker. He was as close to being perfect as any man will ever be."

"The one thing that stands out in my mind is the love that Elvis generated into the world," writes another. "His entire being...those eyes...such deep expressions of love, understanding, patience, kindness. Such a beautiful, spiritual soul eminated from his presence and to this day it hasn't left us...."

In *The Majic Bus*, author Douglas Brinkley is standing at Graceland's Wall of Love when he comes across "a teenage girl with a Magic Marker...busy inscribing something to the King. 'What are you writing?' I asked. Without looking up, she continued scrawling intently. 'I'm asking Elvis to help me find a job.' For some reason, in some warped way, this response made sense to me. It was the cult of Saint Elvis, a powerful intercessor and bearer of deeply felt prayers to a God who wasn't dead."

That notion of "a God who wasn't dead" is certainly apt, but perhaps Brinkley misidentified who that god is. Elvis, it strikes me, is a living spirit, much more like one of the day-to-day deities of many non-Judeo-Christian faiths—Hinduism, Vodun, Santeria, et al.—where the gods are immediately present and interact with the faithful in the most direct and intimate ways.

Mainstream American Protestantism and Catholicism offer something less than a living, day-to-day reality of the sacred. God and his saints are too remote, both historically and spiritually, and Jesus is eternally at the brink of death. As related in the New Testament, Christ's resurrection is an afterthought, the completion of a mythic story cycle tacked on later by early Christians who had learned of it from other cults in the region. In the New Testament the resurrected Christ is a curiously vague figure, not a ghost exactly, but terribly less real than the Jesus who'd lived and died a man. At the risk of blaspheming, his postcrucifixion appearances might even be considered Jesus Sightings.

∎ ∎ ∎

Elvis, as you are watching over us from Heaven above, please know that all of us, your devoted fans, are sending you up our undying, eternal love to last forever and a day!—*Suzy Karsten*

Devotion comes from the heart
And only his fans truly play that part.

So whenever one hears Elvis sing
They know it's for his fans, since
they are the only ones who belong.

That is why we must remember
That his soul will forever sing,
Glory Hallelujia, only Elvis is King!

L. KALACHI

Worshipping Elvis—vulgar, uneducated, tacky, a drug addict, a sexual pervert, a redneck—requires a suspension of disbelief, or rather, a leap of faith, that nonbelievers simply can't fathom.

E's followers *know* all of his faults. They certainly know more about him than most skeptics do. They've heard over and over that he was a mama's boy; that he was lecherous, habitually unfaithful to Priscilla, and perhaps deviant as well; that he abandoned control of his life to others, grossly squandering his talents, was too weak willed to stand up to the Colonel; that he was a spendthrift on an unimaginable scale; that he died fat and drug-addled.

Yet they refuse to let any of that sully their image of him. The E who has become a god is the Good Elvis who loved his mother, sang gospel songs, was charitable and humble and kind. He is the grown-up version of the Elvis remembered by the ladies of Lauderdale Courts who knew him as a youth—"a nice boy, a kind boy, someone both thoughtful and attentive, someone who truly cares" (*Last Train to Memphis*). As early as the late sixties—years before E died—an elderly British man at a rock 'n' roll convention faced a documentary film camera and declared quite simply, "I feel that if more people in the world followed Elvis Presley's way of life, the world would be a much better place."

"What is remarkable about the generation of religious belief," religious historian David Chidester writes, "is not so much that people believe, but that religion provides a situation in which disbelief may be suspended." E's followers are in the process of doing what all personality cults do in the course of becoming full-fledged religions: creating a mythology, emphasizing the good things about the object of their devotion and de-emphasizing the bad, editing, embroidering, no doubt exaggerating, so that the historical figure begins to fade behind the mythological one. This is precisely how the cult of Jesus developed into Christianity. Ultimately it won't matter who "the real Elvis" was, any more than it matters to Christians who "the real Jesus" was. Stories that are useful are passed along; the rest are censored, edited out, and then forgotten. Mythology has its own purpose, quite apart from history.

Elvis' flaws, as many observers and even skeptics have conceded, are what make him an *American* god. Americans have always been democratic about their gods and heroes, on the one hand wanting them to be glorious, unique, and saintly, but simultaneously demanding that they remain plain folk. In this century we've been drawn to many great figures with tragic weaknesses: Babe Ruth, FDR, Douglas MacArthur, JFK, Judy Garland, Elvis, Marilyn, O. J. Simpson, and Kurt Cobain leap to mind. Even if we admire a clearly superior human being—a genius, a saint, or person of extraordinary talent—we root around to discover their flaws, their humanness, their just-like-us-ness. We respected Einstein's genius, but we *liked* him because he was a genius who talked funny, couldn't comb his hair, and wore baggy Princeton sweatshirts.

The Greek legendizers of Homer and Hesiod's time understood that flaws make gods and heroes more approachable. All their gods and heroes had their foibles and shortcomings—they each had their Achilles' heel. Even Zeus was notoriously weak willed and prone to fits of lust, anger, and envy. This makes him a more sympathetic figure—it "humanizes" him. Similarly, the Old Testament Yahweh was a more "human" deity than the Christians' God the Father; he involved himself personally in the affairs of the Jews, was quick to succumb to fits of anger or to display fatherly pride.

Because they have the intermediary figure of Jesus Christ to supply the human element, the Christians allow their concept of God to be more removed, more perfect in all ways. There's no need to humanize Jesus: he was both a god and a man. This role of man-god as sympathetic intercessionary between humans and their supreme deities can be found in many religions and mythologies throughout the world.

In many traditions tragic flaws are linked to the idea that gods must be sacrificed. As sacrificial victims, they become supremely sympathetic figures. We pray both *to* them and *for* them, ask for their protection but also feel compelled to protect them. A strain of victimization prevails in much of Christianity, especially Roman Catholicism. In the history of the Catholic Church, many populist cultic traditions have focused specifically, and often morbidly, on Christ's role not as triumphant savior but as suffering victim, a figure as much of pathos as transcendence. This role is carried over in the gruesome sufferings of many saints and martyrs.

It is this victimized Jesus over whom Christians have always wept and swooned; he who knew pain, fear, and humiliation is the one they feel closest to. In Protestantism as well as Catholicism, it is the victimized Jesus who must be defended and protected from those who would do him harm—the Jews, the pagans, the Satanists, the secular humanists, the godless atheists, the Protestants (for Catholics), the Catholics (for Protestants), and so on. If Jesus hadn't been victimized—if he'd simply lived, shown himself to be a holy man, and passed along peacefully like the Buddha—there might not have been the emotional lynchpin of anger and revenge that has motivated so much Onward-Christian-Soldiers militancy.

Elvis' followers possess a similarly militant resolve to defend and protect E from being victimized by outsiders. Their perception is that outsiders have been out to get Elvis, and them, from the very start.

They may not have witnessed the vicious attacks of the 1950s, but they've never stopped smarting from them. Older fans remember those days and younger ones have seen the documentation: the well-known footage of disc jockeys smashing Elvis records and refusing to play any more of that evil rock 'n' roll; the Jersey City Commissioner of Public Safety banning concerts by Elvis and all rock 'n' rollers because the music was "not for the good of the community." A famous film clip shows a redneck in a small southern town declaring that the menfolk have set up "a twenty-man committee to do away with this vulgar, animalistic, nigger rock and roll bop." They were going into record stores and places with jukeboxes thuggishly demanding that Elvis' records be removed.

The fans' paranoia of the press goes back to the very beginnings of their fandom. Throughout the 1950s the media attacked Elvis with a savagery that has not been equaled since. The *San Francisco Chronicle* wrote him off as being "in appalling taste." *Miami News* columnist Herb Rau blasted him as "the biggest freak in show business history. . . . Elvis can't sing, can't play the guitar—and can't dance." Rau was scandalized by the way Elvis "shakes his pelvis like any striptease babe," and he scorned the fans as "idiots." The *New York Daily News* declared that pop music "has reached its lowest depths in the 'grunt and groin' antics of one Elvis Presley." The paper excoriated Elvis' performance style as an "affront" and "an exhibition that was suggestive and vulgar, tinged with the kind of animalism that should be confined to dives and bordellos." (Animalism? Openly mocking him on national tv, Steve Allen coerced young Elvis into singing "Hound Dog" to a hound dog. Later, in his movies, he'd sing to dogs, cats, even a bull.) The *New York Times* announced that he had "no discernible singing ability . . . caterwauling his unintelligible lyrics in an inadequate voice, during a display of primitive physical movement difficult to describe in terms suitable to a family newspaper." The Catholic paper *America* cried out that "his movements and motions during a performance, described as a 'strip-tease with clothes,' were not only suggestive but downright obscene. The youngsters at the shows . . . literally 'went wild,' some of them actually rolling in the aisles." *Life* simply refused to cover him at all.

Throughout his Hollywood sixties, E's movies were universally derided as lowest-brow kitsch suitable only for audiences of white-trash housewives. His "Comeback" period, beginning in 1968, earned him a little very grudging respect, but that had disappeared by 1973; media coverage of his last years was dominated by the Fat Elvis caricature and, at the very end, by the scandalous revelations of his drug use and strange behavior.

When he died in 1977, the fantastic outpouring of grief around the world took the media by surprise. They responded for a few days or weeks with a crocodilian show of respect. But by the eighties E and his followers were America's favorite cultural joke, the epitome of everything low class, white trash, trailer-parky, hillbilly, and kitschy. The eighties were the years of Elvis' tabloid purgatory, the Elvis Sighting years, a bizarre circus, his most shabby and tawdry era yet.

In the late eighties the tide slowly began to turn. Elvis' followers had not only remained steadfastly faithful but had continued to increase, crossing class lines, nationalities, and generations. Pop-music historians began the inevitable process of reevaluating his impact on world culture and renovating the party line on his music and career. Though Elvis and his followers were still largely objects of jest, the howling ridicule began to soften into something more like ironic nostalgia and even a certain backhanded fondness. By the early 1990s political leaders in the world's two great superpowers could openly declare themselves Elvis fans and win points for it.

This is not to say that the outrages, as Elvists see it, have ceased. As late as June 1994, *The T. C. B. Gazette* of the Looking For Elvis Fan Club in Mobile, Alabama, was calling on all fans to boycott the tabloid *Star*. In an open letter to all fans, Indiana fan Midge Smith wrote that "As Elvis fans, we all feel compelled to protect Elvis from those that profit from his name and image, only to turn the truth into trash." To protest an article in *Star* that did "nothing but belittle Elvis," Smith called the tabloid and spoke to an editor, whom she identifies as Mr. Bob Smith, who insulted the King and "insinuated that the loyalty of Elvis' fans proved only that we are idiots in his eyes.... We informed Mr. Bob Smith that we were going to get the word out to all of Elvis' fans worldwide not to purchase the 'Star' Magazine anymore. Elvis and his fans have been hurt enough with bad publicity.... Elvis' fans are like one big family spread throughout the world, and there is no reason for us to include such people and their stories in our circle. They refuse to recognize and understand Elvis' magical presence and inner beauty, and we should no longer support their cause by paying them to state their falsities and personal opinions." "So please," the fan club's Joan Clark concluded, "BOYCOTT, BOY-COTT, BOYCOTT STAR MAGAZINE NOW! NOW! NOW! NOW! NOW!"

Elvists have had to defend their faith not only from ridiculing outsiders, but from traitorous insiders as well. In 1977 three of Elvis' bodyguards and friends shocked fans and the world when they published *Elvis: What Happened?,* their tell-all exposé of his sex-and-drugs lifestyle. To this day fans refer to it only as "that book," and whereas the rest of Elvis' Memphis Mafia are revered as his disciples, living treasures whose every memory of and anecdote about Elvis, no matter how trivial, is received as scripture, the names of Red West, Sonny West, and Dave Hebler have been all but wiped from Elvist history.

And then there's Priscilla—say *Pri-SSSS-illa.* As the King's queen consort, his wife, and the mother of his only child, she was envied and admired above all women in the Elvist cosmos save his mother. Then she abandoned him, breaking his heart, and became the most reviled. For years she, like Red and Sonny West, was an unperson among Elvists. Yet it was through her savvy management of his estate that Graceland was opened to all and became a world pilgrimage site, so over the years Elvists have grudgingly raised their opinion of her slightly. Still, they've not yet exactly warmed to her or to her corporate bureaucracy at Graceland, whose ultimate control over their sacred pilgrimage site frustrates them.

The fans have also had to endure E's Evil Stepmother, Dee Presley, who married his dad shortly after the death of E's sainted mother. E never liked her, and thus neither have his followers. In 1992 she went to the *National Enquirer* with the shocking claim that the relationship between E and his mother had been incestuous. The storm of outrage from Elvists was best encapsulated in the newsletter of the That's The Way It Is fan club of Chicago:

> Well, here we go again! Another roach has crawled out of the woodwork. This time namely Dee "The Hag" Presley!
>
> We as Elvis fans have always known that this hag who impersonates a human was, from the very beginning, in love with Elvis and only settled for Vernon because it kept her close. It also gave her access to her God which we also know to be Money! She is merely another in a long line of money grubbers who sit around trying to figure out how to outdo the next one in making up the biggest lie. However this time she has stepped over the line. She has TRIED to take something beautiful (Elvis' love for his mom) & make it ugly. And Tried is the word. She has TRIED to do this but the only thing she has succeeded in doing is showing herself to be the low life we have always known her to be, and a pathetic excuse for a human being.
>
> . . . The one thing we think this lie may have put to rest is the fact that our beloved Elvis is gone, because if he wasn't he would have come forward and killed Dee.

The constant need to defend the King and themselves against all the detractors is one of the primary adhesives that gives Elvis' dispersed and increasingly diverse following a sense of community. The notion that only "Elvis' friends" truly appreciate him and everything he did is their version of declaring themselves the King's Chosen People.

"The greatness of Elvis can only be understood by those who appreciate him as I do," fan Mike George writes. "I now have a six-year-old daughter who has started to appreciate and fall for him as I did as a child. My four-year-old son is not far behind. It's wonderful to relive those feelings through my children. Elvis' music will never die. . . ."

"I've always been at the peak of happiness when surrounded in Elvis music and friends," Marge Fossa testifies. "I understand his life and how he gave his life, time, work, love, loyalty to us, his fans. I've always been loyal to him for his outstanding achievements. I've given up jobs, friends, boyfriends (in the 50's) for my love of Elvis. . . ."

"Not only will his music live till the end of time," Craig Blasy declares, "but Elvis the person will live on till the end of the world. Every Elvis fan from the past, present and future deserves a pat on the back for associating themselves with the greatest entertainer that ever lived."

Some aspects of Elvism *are* undeniably preposterous; in some of their odder moments during the Elvis Sighting years, his followers certainly brought ridicule on themselves. But as Holland Cotter wrote in the *New York Times,* "religious thinking is by definition suspect: obscurant, manipulative, suited only for the uneducated and the gullible. . . . It is as if the Victorian fear of sex has been replaced by a modern fear of the sacred." Are look-alike Elvis impersonators in identical white jumpsuits and paste-on sideburns inherently goofier than look-alike Chasidic Jews in identical frock coats and hats? Why should a pilgrimage to Graceland be considered an indisputably kitschier pursuit than a pilgrimage to Lourdes or Mecca?

■　■　■

His spirit in our hearts today,
Guides us through each passing day.
The joy of love, the joy of laughter,
He will live forever after.

TARA LYNN

I reached out my hand and Elvis took it.
He showed me the way to a better day,
He Touched Me.
His way took away the dismay,
He gave me the faith
to strive for the best and leave the rest . . .

MEGAN MURPHY

He gave us love and joy and hope to last all our lives long.
He lives in heaven now, but we still love him so . . .

CARLA CRAIG

How many Elvist true believers are there in the world? Who
are they? Where are they? No one calls himself an "Elvist."
There are no official Elvist churches where believers can attend
services, no baptismal rites or Church of Elvis registries. Elvism
is entirely self-generated and grass roots, a populist worship in
the most fundamental sense. At this stage it is entirely innocent
of an articulated theology, because it has no central authority,
no college of Elvist cardinals to write it. Elvists simply are
acting on a basic human instinct to worship.

Over a billion Elvis records have been sold worldwide.
Over a billion people watched his 1973 tv special, "Aloha from
Hawaii." It would be conservative to suppose there are tens of
millions of people in the world who would at least call themselves fans of E's music.

Roughly three quarters of a million people visit Graceland
annually. Some forty thousand of them visit during the Elvist

High Holy Days in August; of them, ten to twenty thousand participate in the most solemn ritual, the Candlelight Vigil and procession on the eve of Elvis' death. How many true believers are among them? Factoring out the tourists and curiosity seekers, the disinterested spouses and children, the dedicated fans with no religious or spiritual inclinations, how many true Elvists are in that procession? A few thousand? How many more are there around the world?

Elvis fan clubs are the nodes of his followers' worldwide network. There are fan clubs in big cities and small towns throughout the Americas, Europe (England claims some of the oldest and largest anywhere), and Asia (predictably, Japanese clubs are particularly active and well organized). Fan clubs have been secretly organized in nations where they were specifically prohibited by government, including the Soviet Union and Pakistan. Fan clubs originated and mobilize the great pilgrimages to Memphis, both in August (on the anniversary of E's death) and in January (to celebrate the King's birthday), and it's with the fan clubs that corporate Graceland negotiates and coordinates its ever-growing calendar of official events during those pilgrimages. The fan clubs network among themselves on other local, national, and international gatherings during the year. Working both individually and collectively, the fan clubs do good works and fundraise in Elvis' name. It was through the fan-club network that the Elvis postage stamp became a reality. And the fan clubs act as a communications net, spreading the news and keeping the faith in all matters Elvisian.

For all that, there's no agreement even on how many fan clubs there are. In 1994 corporate Graceland officially estimated some 370 fan clubs worldwide. But Darwin Lamm, publisher of *Elvis International Forum*—the flagship of Elvis fan magazines and an invaluable source of insights into the Elvist mentality (including many of the quotes in this book)—tells me that he considers no more than 160 of these to be "real" fan clubs, with active memberships of fifteen or more people. The largest of these fan clubs count their members in the thousands, but there is some question about these numbers as well. The largest fan club in England claims ten thousand members, of which Lamm believes no more than a thousand are really active participants.

Fan clubs can give the impression that they are made up entirely of middle-aged housewives, older widows, and spinsters. Like most stereotypes, there's a grain of truth in this. At any Elvis gathering it is the fan-club ladies, in their identical club t-shirts and hairdos, who seem to dominate, busying themselves with arrangements, running the Make-A-Wish Foundation raffle tables, forming the hostess brigade. They are Elvism's "church ladies," and they give it its reputation as the quintessential modern coterie cult.

In fact, though, the fan clubs, like Elvis' following in general, are far more diverse than they might at first appear. Many club founders and presidents are men, and all fan clubs assert that their memberships range across all ages, usually representing two or three generations. Brett Mallard, founder of New Hampshire's fan club, wrote to *Elvis International Forum:* "It was said from the beginning that Elvis would be a flash in the pan. It was just a phase, and the kids would get over it. . . . Forty years after Elvis' introduction to the world, and sixteen years after his death, look around and see who worships the 'King of Rock and Roll.' It's not just the graying, overweight men and women who grew up with Elvis in the fifties. Today, more than ever, Elvis Presley's fans span the generations. In our fan club alone, we have members that range from six years old to people in their 70's. I can relay many stories of the young fans I've met since being introduced to the 'Elvis World'. . . . It was the kids that started the legacy, and it will be the kids that will continue Elvis' legacy. Just ask my 11-year-old son, Brandon. . . ."

My observations at Graceland and other Elvis gatherings confirm Mallard's assertions. Whatever it is, Elvism has been passed down from its apostolic founding generation.

"On the day Elvis passed away, I was only a few months past six years old," says Kelly Wright. "Although I do not have many recollections of that day, Elvis still has had a major impact on my life. . . .

"Why I love Elvis so much still remains a mystery to me. I was not even born yet during the times of his greatest achievements and was very young at the time of his death. I never had the opportunity of meeting him or seeing him in concert and, unfortunately, I never will. When I look at his pictures—that smile, those eyes—they all speak of love. . . . The best thing I found in Elvis is a friend, someone you can trust and depend on. . . ."

Henrik Scheutz, a Swedish fan, relates: "Though I am only 22 it feels like I've loved Elvis all my life. I have always been very lonely, so when I haven't had any other friends, I've always had Elvis. Though I never had the chance to meet him, I think I know him better than anybody else.

"We have so much in common; no sisters or brothers, like him, I am humble and shy, and I don't act and dress like everybody else. . . . I just can't imagine a life without Elvis. He will always be my friend."

The fan clubs are by definition the loci of Elvis devotion. But as with Elvis' general following, it would be difficult to pinpoint when devout fandom shades into worship. In 1993 *Reader's Digest* quoted a fan-club president saying that the clubs were "kind of like different churches," in the sense that they compete to demonstrate who's the most devoted. "People worry about who's the No. 1 fan. . . . The new fan club will say the old one wasn't putting Elvis first."

Fan-club publications, from the glossy *Elvis International Forum* to the humblest typewritten one-sheet, are often characterized by the same protesting-too-much conflict of faith J. D. Sumner exhibits. On one page of a newsletter, a fan will write one of those "Elvis was a man, not a god, though he was very godlike" statements. On the next page, there will be an entry like this letter from Micheline Verdiere, of the Elvis TCB Fan Club in Belgium, to all her friends in the Elvis That's The Way It Is Fan Club of Chicago: "Dear friends, our LOVE and RESPECT for Elvis are unlimited . . . and we are in touch in full appreciation of our personal battle to do the best for Elvis. . . . Let's continue to work hard for him, because his LIGHT on our world today is the guarantee to give HOPE and PEACE for the next generations. . . . *We believe in Elvis just like we believe in GOD* . . . and I'm sure that we are on the right way. "

This epistle to her distant brothers and sisters in faith brings us to another analogy with Christianity. The very first Christians were a personality cult—a small group of fans, let's say, of an extraordinarily charismatic speaker. For decades after the death of Christ, Christians didn't call themselves "Christians," nor did they think of themselves as members of an identified Church. They were Jews, Gentiles, and pagans attracted to a figure named Jesus. They were widely dispersed in small groups, at first in the eastern Mediterranean, then spreading west into the heart of the Roman empire. They were a kind of pen-pal network of a few far-flung believers keeping in touch and gradually defining their faith through word of mouth and through epistles carried from town to town.

Developing their beliefs in the absence of any central authority, the dispersed chapters of the new faith were prone to schism and competitive bickering. By the time they began to write the scriptures that would be known as the New Testament, many decades after Jesus' death, most details of his actual life had become lost or obscured behind an accretion of legend, folklore, miracle tales, mythology, and eschatological ruminations.

In Rome, which would become the center of the Christian world, there were no Christian churches for the first three centuries of the cult's growth and development. When they weren't being banned and persecuted by the state, Roman Christians were ridiculed by their neighbors. Graffiti scrawled on the walls of a second-century boys' gymnasium lampoons Jesus as an ass hung on a cross. Not surprisingly, Roman Christians met privately in their homes. Their chief ritual was a simple shared meal, which eventually became the Mass. The first Christian basilica wasn't built until after Constantine issued the Edict of Milan in 313.

By then, of course, the Jesus cult had grown into a full-fledged Church of Jesus, the official state religion of the West.

It took three hundred years. Elvism has had, at the time of this writing, seventeen years.

■ ■ ■

Beautiful memories, memories of a wonderful man that God saw as special and gifted him with talents that most of us can only dream of. . . . Because God knew Elvis would be the one who would share his talents with the rest of us, and make this world a happier place to be.
—*Marie Bleecker*

Will Elvism become a full-fledged religion? Most cults don't. For every faith actively practiced today, untold numbers of cults, sects, and religions have dissolved. Some lasted only as long as their founders; others flourished for centuries or millennia only to die out with the cultures that practiced them.

Then again, new cults, sects, and religions are created all the time. This seems difficult to grasp for people who are used to thinking that there are a half dozen great world religions and a scattering of also-rans and oddities. Elvism has already survived and grown far beyond what anyone expected of it ten years ago. It has already negotiated the crucial step of passing from generation to generation. It has spread across barriers of class, ethnicity, and nationality as well. Slowly, organically, it is building its own structures and codes. Elvists' awareness of themselves as a "church" may come later. So may the theology, although plenty of belief systems thrive with little theology or philosophy; many are little more than attempts to evoke good luck, or are maintained as traditions of ritualized behavior without a great deal of thought behind them.

Popular religion is a lot more about *feeling* than *thinking* anyway. Joseph Campbell put it well: "People say that what we're all seeking is a meaning for life. I don't think that's what we're really seeking. I think that what we're seeking is an experience of being alive, so that our life experiences on the purely physical plane will have resonances within our innermost being and reality, so that we actually feel the rapture of being alive."

As I've worked on this book, I've been asked a hundred times, "Does the world really need another book about Elvis?" While much has been written about the religiosity of Elvis' following, only a few articles and books have dealt with the indisputable phenomenon of the growing Elvis faith. I don't pray to Elvis. But I don't pray to any gods or hold the beliefs of any religion. Maybe that's why I find other people's religions interesting. And Elvism offers me the opportunity to observe the process of a religion creating itself and its god. This book is based on my watching and thinking about this process.

R E T U R N
T O   Z E N D A

. . . I do hope you will read this letter and consider publishing it. It may help others to read that their problems can be overcome with enough faith.

For years I have wanted to attend [Tribute Week] and go to Graceland, but, you see, for the past 20 years I have suffered with anxiety attacks; so each year I would cancel out. . . .

From the moment I reached its walls, I could feel the love and peace all around me. My first night I went to the Meditation Gardens and cried and said my thanks to Elvis. I was truly at peace with myself for the first time in a long time. . . . There is something special about the place and you can feel "his" presence there. . . .

"A True Elvis Fan"

I N THE LOBBY of a Ramada Inn near Memphis International Airport, Elvis Week, 1994:
"Mommy, I saw Elvis."
"Did you."
"Yes, but he's gone."

■ ■ ■

At Graceland Plaza, the all-Elvis shopping center across the street from the estate, two middle-aged American women in pink fan-club t-shirts are trying to converse with two young German women in their own fan-club's outfits. The Americans don't speak a word of German and the Germans speak surprisingly little English. Confusion. Then one of the Americans turns to her friend and says, "I know, do 'Love Me Tender' in sign language." Her friend signs the first few lines, reciting the accompanying words slowly and loudly. The German girls watch her hands, smiling, and look totally mystified.

In the shops, you can buy Elvis anything. Elvis wall clocks, Elvis mugs, bisque Elvises, plastic Elvises, Elvis pins, ties, earrings, ashtrays, pens, refrigerator magnets, license-plate holders, commemorative plates, music boxes, musical teddy bears, Christmas cards, posters, books, t-shirts, toy guitars, silk jackets, caps, CDs, videos, socks, scarves, sunglasses, pillows, key rings, calendars, shot glasses, shampoo, perfume, oil paintings, reproductions of his gold and platinum records, laminated repros of his driver's license and birth certificate, copies of his will. I've heard about little vials containing Elvis' sweat, but I don't see any. I do find the Elvis nail clippers a friend requested.

In the parking lot, under a tent, they're showing Elvis films nonstop on a wide-screen tv. *Aloha from Hawaii*, giant Elvis, in glistening white jumpsuit, pumped, at the height of his powers, whipping through "Suspicious Minds," broadcast via satellite to a billion or more people around the world.

The lobby of the visitor center that's the staging area for Graceland tours has an exhibition of Elvis art. Oil paintings, charcoals and pastels, drawings and sculptures of sultry, androgynous Elvises with long lashes and pouty red lips, a naked and nymphy Elvis leaning up against a tree, a sexy satanic Elvis. A saintly or godlike Elvis hovers in the sky of a heavenly blue-lit

Graceland, as the faces of Vernon and Gladys, his mom and dad, gaze down from the clouds.

A painting labeled "Elvis' Brazilians Friends" is a naive copy of the *Aloha from Hawaii* album cover. It depicts the Aloha Elvis as a colossus standing up over the blue planet, the Telstar satellite over his shoulder projecting visible beams, transmitting his message to the whole world. A section of little kids' artworks shows Elvis portraits with words scrawled on them like "Elvis is good," "Elvis was a honorary Policeman," and "Elvis like to play the good tar."

A quick review of license plates in the lot covers a quarter of the United States: FL, MN, WA, CA, TX, NM, ME, KS, VA, AL, MO, MI. There is a consul's car from D. C. Signs in the windows or soaped onto the doors: "Graceland or Bust," "Destination: Graceland," the inevitable "Honk if you love Elvis."

■ ■ ■

Every evening, when the paid tours are over, Graceland stays open for two hours so you can walk up the hill for free and spend some private time with E in the Meditation Garden. It's off to one side of the house, just past the kidney-shaped swimming pool. A circular fountain, a columned portico, a stone wall with backlit stained-glass windows depicting scenes of, I guess, the Holy Land. In the ground at one side of the fountain, behind a knee-high wrought-iron railing, six-foot bronze plaques lie flat on the ground marking E's grave, Vernon's, Gladys', and his grandmother Minnie Mae's, and there is a little plaque for his twin brother Jesse Garon, who died at childbirth and was buried in Tupelo.

It's 8 P.M., Thursday. I landed at Memphis airport an hour ago and dropped my bags at the airport Red Roof Inn, where the young black woman at the desk was tied up on the phone with someone demanding a room. "We don't *have* any rooms, ma'am. It's *Elvis Week*." I rushed over to visit the Meditation Garden before closing time at 8:30.

It's early in Elvis Week, aka Tribute Week, and the crowds won't pour in until tomorrow and the next day. About thirty people are in the Meditation Garden, sitting on the low semi-circular steps facing the graves. Quiet, respectful, half of them are middle-aged fan-club ladies in their uniform t-shirts, but half are young people who just look, well, regular. They whisper to each other or stare silently at E's grave and the eternal flame that flickers in a glass case at the head of the grave as they slap at the fountain-bred mosquitoes whose wings sizzle in the hot night air.

The young people just sit on the steps, looking self-conscious, like young people at a funeral, waiting for someone older to show them how to act. A middle-aged woman, the only black person there, takes the lead. She gets up slowly, goes to the railing, kneels at E's grave and begins to pray, sometimes unfolding her hands to pass one palm flat in the air over the foot of the plaque, a kind of comforting gesture. The young people fall silent. Over in the shadows, the security guards' radios sputter.

Towering off to one side is a big white statue of Jesus; chiseled into the base, with unintended irony, is the name PRESLEY. I'm thinking this must be the statue that was struck and scarred by a bolt of lightning; Elvis understood this to be a sign from God and later adopted the lightning bolt as his TCB ("Taking Care of Business—In a Flash") symbol. I found out later that the Jesus statue wasn't placed here until 1977, after his death— his father had it moved here from the family cemetery plot a few miles away.

A fan-club lady stands before it, looking quietly distraught, gazing up into the face, speaking to it in a low murmur. Is she speaking to Jesus, or E? A couple of security guards stand in the shadows nearby, keeping an eye on her, their radios occasionally crackling. Off to the other side is a tract of fenced-in pasture where Graceland's four handsome riding horses snuffle the grass and switch their tails at the mosquitoes. They come up to the fence and blink big, damp eyes at me.

I head back down the hill to Elvis Presley Boulevard. Fans call the two-block length of stone wall that borders the front of the estate the Wall of Love. Long before Elvis died they used it as a kind of message board, magic markering notes to him and to one another. Nothing big or graffiti-gaudy: small, handwritten, private notes, a few small drawings of E, crude and mutely ingenuous as the figures scratched into the walls of Pompeii.

The entire length of the wall is covered with tens of thousands of these notes, new ones layered over old ones. The wall gets scrubbed clean every year or so, and new messages begin to appear instantly. Besides English, I see ones in French, German, Spanish, Kanji, something Scandinavian, something Eastern European, notes by people from Mexico, Cuba, Quebec.

Elvis lives in us.

There is only one King and we know who he is.

Elvis, regular people may think you're dead but you will always be alive in our hearts.

Elvis, you are my bridge over troubled waters.

Elvis, it took 20 years to get here. Next stop, heaven.

Elvis, I finally made it. You'll be with me always.

■   ■   ■

On the tv in my room at the Red Roof Inn, Woodstock '94 is all over the news. I did Woodstock once, in 1969, and never felt a need to do it again. Elvis Week is something I've wanted to do for years.

I didn't much give a damn about Elvis in 1969, and I wasn't moved much by his death in '77. But the very first record I ever bought was "Hound Dog." I was five years old, and my sister, five years older, got me and my brother to pitch in a quarter each to buy it. I remember jumping around on our beds when she played it on her little portable turntable, but I don't remember if we actually liked the song. The first Elvis song I remember liking was "Return to Sender," when I was ten or so. It was only later in my teen years that I found out the title was not in fact "Return to Zenda."

Like many people, from some of E's most faithful followers to hipster ironists, I really only became fascinated with Elvis years after his death, and then it was not so much Elvis himself that interested me, but Elvism, the extraordinary Elvis phenomena—the sightings, the pilgrimages, the shrines, the incredible permutations of his afterlife as one of the immortals. You could like that or hate it, find it bizarre or just ignore it, but it was there, it was everywhere, an authentic and in many ways admirably defiant expression of global populist culture. I was fascinated by the grass-roots tenacity of it. Gradually, as I learned more about Elvis, learned to listen to the music, I became a fan. What I experienced was a retroactive nostalgia: I found myself embracing the cultural product that, despised as kitsch when it was current, had now become a cult totem.

Something on the order of seven hundred thousand people visited Graceland in 1994, making it the most visited home in the U. S. after the White House. Graceland staff people tell me that during the height of the season, June through September, they receive about twenty thousand visitors a week; for Elvis Week '94, seventeen years after his death, the crowd is estimated at forty thousand—twenty-four tour groups an hour, eight hours a day, seven days a week.

Graceland has been a pilgrimage site for Elvis fans and curiosity seekers since the day Elvis moved in. On August 16, 1977, when the news of his death was broadcast, they began to pour in from all over the country. Between thirty and sixty thousand people massed outside the gate over the next few days.

His body was originally placed in a mausoleum, near that of his mother, Gladys, at Forest Hill cemetery, a few miles from the estate. Some sources claim that as many as one million people visited the cemetery in the first month he was there. After an attempt to rob the mausoleum, security concerns led Vernon to have Elvis and Gladys moved to the Memorial Garden that October.

The fans started Elvis Week in 1978, when a handful of them showed up at the gate on August 15 to observe the first anniversary of his death. A few of them—five, according to Elvis lore—lit candles and placed them atop the wall. They sang some Elvis songs and kept watch all night.

It was during this first anniversary that a fan pointed her camera at some cumulus clouds over Graceland and snapped them forming a giant profile of Elvis. Like those tabloid photos of Jesus or Satan in the clouds, this photo really *does* look an awful lot like E. "I guess in a way this just testifies to the fact that Elvis was watching what was going on at Graceland," the woman beatifically told an interviewer in the 1984 video documentary *Mondo Elvis*.

More fans visited the next year, and the next. When Graceland went corporate and opened for tours in the early 1980s, management started to get involved in organizing a burgeoning week-long schedule of events.

The tenth anniversary in 1987 marked a high point for news coverage. (It's no coincidence that sightings and other strange phenomena reached all-time highs over the next couple of years.) But the fans aren't drawn to Graceland by the media. The two questions I am most frequently asked during Elvis Week are a politely suspicious "Where y'all from?" and the more direct "You aren't going to mock us, are you?"

．　■　．

In the 95-plus heat, the swampy, flood-plain smell of mud pervades the entire town of Memphis, and everyone moves slow and heavy-lidded through it, like gator people. As any Memphibian will tell you, there are decidedly two sides of the tracks in Memphis. On the right side of the tracks, the folks of middle-class establishment Memphis would just as soon Elvis had never happened. They seem much more comfortable characterizing Memphis as Beale Street, Home of the Blues. Memphis, for all that Elvis has done to make it, literally and figuratively, an American Mecca, is less than warmly hospitable to his fans.

Graceland is well over on the wrong side of the tracks, in low-class Memphis, out by the airport and highways lined with honky tonks and motels and Shoneys and Dennys, car dealer lots and truck repair lots, the massive industrial property that's FedEx's global nerve center, and some of the very nastiest, scariest-looking topless bars I've seen anywhere. Graceland management has erected a billboard on Memphis' beltway visible as you pass the airport: a glowing photographic portrait of E that beckons "Welcome to My World" and gives directions on how to get there. It's there because there's no official highway sign marking the exit for Graceland—a graphic indication of the depth of official lack of appreciation, or at least some highway official's disgust.

Before moving into Graceland, Elvis did in fact try to cross the tracks. In 1956 he bought his first house for himself and his parents, a rancher on Audobon Drive in a middle-class Memphis suburb of doctors, lawyers, and businessmen. Within months, the neighbors were complaining about the constant traffic he was attracting on their quiet streets, the twenty-four-hour-a-day crowds of teenagers and reporters who were trampling their well-kept lawns. They turned up their noses when Gladys hung laundry to dry in her backyard. A neighborhood committee asked Elvis to move; he responded with an offer to buy all their houses. They refused. Stung by their snooty attitude, Elvis soon bought Graceland, a house Gladys had spotted over in lower-class Memphis.

So most of Elvis Week takes place outside of Memphis proper, out in the boondocks around the airport. There are collectors' sales in the lobbies and meeting rooms of the Ramada Inn and Econo-Lodge, concerts in a banquet room of the airport Best Western, impersonator performances on a makeshift stage in the parking lot of the Elvis Presley Boulevard Shoney's (which has an all-Elvis jukebox inside that gives you unlimited free plays). Watching the Norwegian fans, the French, the Elvis Fan Club of Japan shuttling in buses and vans from one motel to the other, I wonder how many of them know they've been ghettoized. Some of them don't see Memphis proper at all.

Then again, Memphis proper is, to paraphrase southern soul singer Clarence Carter, a sixty-minute city. There's Beale Street, with its handful of blues clubs and a nice little storefront museum. The wide brown swirl of the Mississippi, and the aptly, prosaically named Mud Island out in the middle of it.

The grandest structure in the city, far more grand than Graceland, is the giant mirrored-glass Pyramid on the riverbanks. Inside it's just another arena for indoor sports and concerts, but from the outside it adds quite a mystical element to the city's otherwise drab skyline, its sloping glass sides glistening silver in the miasmal river-town heat.

Memphis, the city of Pharaohs. A poorly reproduced statue of Pharaoh Ramses II stands stiff guard at the Pyramid's street entrance. In his sloping Pharaoh's headcloth, with his hieratically-limned eyes and his full-cheeked, full-lipped pout, he bears some resemblance to E wearing his Valentino-style sheik's headcloth, his eyes hieratically mascaraed, his lips in full pout, in *Harum Scarum*. Priscilla's wedding-day Nefertiti-Cleopatra makeup and hairdo comes to mind; it looked as though he were marrying the Queen of the Nile (or, as things turned out, his Queen of Denial). It's remarkable that Hollywood never cast them as Pharaoh Elvis and Queen Nefertiti Priscilla in a *Ten Commandments*–scale epic.

When a reporter from the *Los Angeles Times* visited the Pyramid gift shop in 1987, he was tickled to find postcards of Ramses sharing a rack with postcards of Elvis. He asked the young lady behind the counter if that wasn't an odd juxtaposition. " 'Not at all,' she replied graciously, amused that anybody should ask such a question. 'They're both kings!' "

In Memphis in August, the Pyramid burns bright as chrome. It shimmies on rising waves of heat and humidity and seems to levitate above the other buildings. It reminds me of an advertisement I saw for the 1994 "Exclusive International Phonecard Series" targeted at Elvis fans, a deluxe set of phonecards printed with various Elvis likenesses, an Elvis picture-disc LP, and other collector items. The corporate logo for the product is an adaptation of the eye-in-the-pyramid image familiar from the back of the U. S. $1 bill. In this logo, however, the eye in the pyramid is the eye of Elvis, heavily mascaraed and exotic looking as the eye of Ramses, the eye of a blue and dancing Krishna, the eye of Yahweh or Leviathan or Moby Dick. The flank of the pyramid that faces the viewer is surprinted with a stylized crown symbolizing his Kingship in no uncertain terms. It is an astonishing fusion of symbolism and iconography that signifies in many directions at once: Freemasonry, Pharaonic Egypt, the Kabbalah, the (almighty) dollar . . . and Elvis the King. Pure marketing that taps directly and unashamedly into Elvist mysticism.

At Graceland's corporate office, a small red-brick building next door to the estate, the Muzak is nonstop Elvis. I ask the receptionist, a dazzlingly efficient and flawlessly cheerful young black woman, if she ever gets sick of hearing it. "Oh nooo," she laughs. "I *love* Elvis. I *wake up* to Elvis."

Corporate Graceland and Elvis Presley Enterprises are a well-oiled tourism-publicity-merchandising machine. I first contacted Graceland several months earlier to request press access to the grounds for Tribute Week. Because it doesn't need much help from the press, and the press, especially print, has never been of much help anyway, I was treated with, let's say, guarded courtesy. It must be what dealing with the Vatican press office is like. By letter, fax, and telephone, I was bounced from Memphis to Graceland's contracted press relations outfit in Los Angeles. No one was rude or unhelpful, but no one was turning cartwheels that a New York journalist was interested in writing about Tribute Week. They probed me about my intentions and attitude. Was I coming to make fun? Or would I write something respectful?

Mentioning that I'm interested in the religiosity of Elvis' cult didn't help. Corporate Graceland and EPE take a dim view of the religiosity of Elvis' cult. They're professional tourism managers, merchandisers of memorabilia, licensers of recordings, videos, publications. The staff is polite with E's more devout fans and helps them coordinate their Tribute Week observances, but they like to stress that the really devoted followers make up a small percentage of visitors, the bulk being merely casual tourists. They clearly feel that it wouldn't be best for the tourism to emphasize Graceland's role as a meeting place for some kind of religious kooks. My observations during Tribute Week make me think they're wrong about this. Many of the casual tourists, at least during Elvis

Week, are drawn to Graceland explicitly to witness the devout Elvists at their ceremonies.

I commit another faux pas when I mention that beyond an article I may be writing an Elvis book. "Who isn't?" they shrug. Officially, Graceland doesn't cooperate with books Graceland hasn't licensed. But I do get a special tour—not VIP, more like MIP (Medium Important Person)—wedged in between two large tour groups. My tour guide, Angie, has worked at Graceland for five years since her family moved to Memphis from Florida. She's an excellent guide, good with trivia, like knowing which two Dylan songs Elvis sang ("It Ain't Me, Babe" and "Tomorrow Is a Long Time").

In 1853 when, after much hardship and hazard, the adventurer Sir Richard Burton reached Muhammad's tomb, the Masjid al-Nabawi, in Medina, he reports that he "was astonished at the mean and tawdry appearance of a place so universally venerated in the Moslem world." He had expected that the final resting place of the founder of one of the world's great religions would be a grand and imposing monument. Instead, he found a small and rather dowdy structure in a cramped courtyard at the center of a warren of dark and narrow alleys. "The longer I looked at it," he recalls, "the more it suggested the resemblance of a museum of second-rate art, an old Curiosity-shop, full of ornaments that are not accessories, and decorated with pauper splendour."

Like some of the world's other great pilgrimage sites— Stonehenge, the Sphinx, the Kaaba in Mecca—Graceland also looms much larger in the imagination than it does on the ground. I wouldn't call it dinky, but it's a stretch to call it a mansion. It's just a biggish, handsome Southern Colonial suburban home with nothing very distinguishing except for the famous gates E designed for the front driveway. The property itself is quite stately, with a decorous treed hill and close-cropped lawn that makes a dignified rise up to the house.

The interior is familiar to thousands from official Graceland postcards and books. I had read that most of the rooms are surprisingly small, and they are. Descriptions of the decor as outrageously tacky are, however, exaggerated. It is true that green shag carpet lines some of the ceilings and that the stairwell to the basement is a dizzying hall of mirrors. There's the infamous Jungle Room, and the long living room, with attached music room, that together give an impression of faux high kitsch grandeur reminiscent of a funeral parlor suite designed by Liberace. Yes, they're tacky, but not as wildly so as I'd been led to believe. Just about any interior decor from the seventies, if frozen in time the way Graceland's is, would look pretty kitschy today. If anything, I'm disappointed that it's not wackier. As bad taste goes, I've seen funnier and uglier.

There's something heartwarming about the lack of taste and design skill and the cramped intimacy of the layout. This is not the King of the World's palace. It is not the Taj Mahal or the Great Pyramid or the White House; it is not even on a scale with, say, the Nixon Library & Birthplace, Nixon's Taj Mahal to himself. It's just a home. You can picture any moderately comfortable middle-class family of the 1970s—a doctor's family, a midlevel bank executive's—living there. It feels lived in. It's like they've all gone off for a week's vacation at Disneyland and tidied up before they left, because a neighbor would be dropping by to bring in the mail. A *Reader's Digest* article once remarked, "It is as though Graceland is waiting; as though Elvis has gone off for a gig in Las Vegas and is due back, maybe tonight."

The tour includes only five of Graceland's twenty-three rooms, all on the ground floor and in the basement; the rest is sealed off to visitors and staff alike, the inner sanctum, the holiest of holies, like the interior of the Kaaba. Tour guides are reduced to constructions like "Elvis' bedroom is said to be at the top of the stairs to the left."

On one wall there's a remarkable oil painting Elvis commissioned in 1969 from the schlock portraitist-to-the-rich-and-famous Ralph Wolfe Cowan, who also did the Reagans, Pope John Paul II, Princess Grace, and JFK. Nearly life-size, it shows Elvis in a glowing Young God pose, looking fit, trim, and eternally in his mid-twenties (a flattering portraitist's conceit, even in 1969). In a saintly, sexy pure white outfit, a jaunty white bandana at his neck, hip cocked, and one thumb hooked in his pants pocket, Elvis stands in the sky amid a gold-drenched hallelujah chorus cathedral of cumulus clouds. Mounted in a gilt frame, it is hung high on the wall so that Elvis seems to gaze down at you from upon high, his expression distant and dreamy, his full lips in a beguilingly enigmatic half-smile, an expression somewhere between his famous sneer and a Mona Lisa simper. You can't help but think *Elvis in heaven* as you gape up at him, and it's no wonder that some fans believe the legend—no doubt discouraged by Graceland staff—that touching the frame can bring blessings and miraculous healing cures.

Elvis built the Trophy Room, a long, narrow extension to Graceland, to hold all his awards. One aisle of display cases is filled with his gold and platinum records. Lapsing into the kind of religious metaphor you don't often hear from Graceland management, Todd Morgan, the director of communications, has called this "the conversion room." In 1992 RCA and the Record Industry Association of America completed an audit updating the accounts of Elvis' total record sales in the United States, and in a ceremony Graceland was presented with 110 gold and platinum albums and singles. (As a point of comparison, Elvis' nearest competition, the Beatles, amassed half as many.) The records are enshrined as a floor-to-ceiling "Wall of Gold" in the racquetball building Elvis had built next to the house in 1975.

It is indeed an awesome sight. Angie drops some heavy statistics: in his first four years, Elvis sold fifty million records; in his fifth year alone, he sold another twenty-five million. In 1984, when he was seven years dead, it was estimated that sales had reached one billion units worldwide. As of 1992, no fewer than forty-eight Elvis recordings had gone gold or platinum *since he died.*

Record collectors and aficionados would point out that the recording industry is notoriously loose in its accounts of sales figures. The multiplicity of formats (LP, EP, and singles on vinyl; CD; cassette and eight-track tape; and boxed set reissue) creates confusion and inaccuracy. Sales outside the domestic United States market—which in Elvis' case are judged to be enormous by any reckoning—are inefficiently tracked. Few experts doubt that Elvis' recordings achieved the billion-unit sales figure, but they note that it is at best an estimate—and possibly a serious *underestimate.* Flaws in and changes to the system for awarding gold and platinum status further confuse the issue.

All this statistical ambiguity hardly blunts the visual impact of that Wall of Gold. In the tour group just ahead, three short, stocky young men dressed as fifties-era Elvises—greasy black ducktails and sideburns, draped jackets and pegged pants, their pastel shirts open wide at the neck to show gold chains dangling in their black chest hair—stand in awe. They lean their pompadoured heads together and murmur what I take to be appreciative comments in some Eastern European tongue.

To knowledgeable fans, there could be no more fitting site for the Wall of Gold than the racquetball building. A two-story cube, it has the high, boxy volume of a mausoleum. It is in the racquetball court that E made his last living appearance on earth. Sometime before dawn on Tuesday, August 16, 1977, he played a little desultory racquetball with his cousin and confidante Billy Smith, Billy's wife, Jo, and his last girlfriend, Ginger Alden. Afterward they relaxed around the upright piano in the adjoining lounge area. I watch two ladies in fan-club t-shirts bend to place their fingertips on the rolled-and-pleated piano bench where Elvis sat as he played and sang "Unchained Melody" and "Blue Eyes Crying in the Rain." He may have taken a drink from the nearby wall-mounted water fountain, which is duly pointed out as an "original fixture" the King may have touched—perhaps even with his lips!—during his final hours. Then, around 7 A.M., he and Ginger retired to his bedroom; she woke up and found him dead on the bathroom floor that afternoon.

■ ■ ■

"We're not here to be Elvis," a Georgia Elvis impersonator named Steve tells the audience of about five hundred fans at Headliners, a big old shed of a dance hall hosting the eighth annual Images Of Elvis World Championship Impersonator Contest. "We're not here to mock Elvis. We're here to pay tribute to his memory."

Big applause from the crowd. Around the hall, six or seven fellow Elvii watch him through their trademark E sunglasses and nod approvingly.

"I don't know about you people," a New York Elvi announces during his performance, "but I am *sick* and *tired* of all the de*rog*atory remarks about Elvis. The jelly donut, spare tire, old man comments. . . . Elvis was forty-two when he died. Is forty-two old? He *was* forty-two, and he will always *be* forty-two."

Never have I seen so many Elvii, or so many different kinds of Elvii, as at Headliners. At times there are up to a dozen Elvii scattered around the room, posing for snapshots, autographing programs, smoking, eyeing the competition, drinking Zima. (The official sponsor, Zima is consumed in nauseous quantities the first night I'm there. By the time I go back two nights later, everyone has switched to beer.)

There are tall, handsome hunk Elvii in homemade white jumpsuits. Short, fat Elvii who look more like Roy Orbison.

Young fifties-era rockabilly Elvii like those Eastern European men I saw at Graceland. An Elvis with a serious underbite. A British Elvi with a Cockney accent thick as Stilton. A slender, cute-as-a-bug Vietnamese Elvi, a third-year med student who says his goal is "to bring Elvis to all the world" and nobody tells him it's already been done. A black Elvi, a female Elvi, a prepubescent Elvi. Elvii from the states of Washington, California, Missouri, New York. A guy from Key West representing a group calling itself the Snorkeling Elvises.

At a rate of about four Elvii per hour, they take turns on the stage, going through their four or five best Elvis tunes. A few of them are very good. Most of them aren't. The crowd responds politely anyway. The crowd, after all, has come to Memphis from all over the United States and beyond to be near E. At Headliners, they can be near multiple Elvises every night, 4 P.M. to 3 A.M., for the entire week. By the time the winner is chosen, I'm told, 250 to 350 Elvii will have performed.

"I want to thank you for being friends of mine," Steve tells the crowd, "and for being friends of Elvis." Like much of what one hears during Tribute Week, this is code. E's true believers do not like to be called "fans." They consider themselves far more than mere fans of Elvis—half the world's population, they'll tell you, are *fans* of Elvis. They call themselves "friends of Elvis." A Society of Friends, you might say.

Despite his jumpsuit, Steve doesn't look a whit like the King. He's middle-aged, roundly paunchy, with a beaky face, thinning hair, and no sideburns. He looks like a dentist or a podiatrist. He looks, frankly, ridiculous.

The four-piece house band starts to vamp the intro to "Poke Salad Annie," a staple of Elvis' seventies tours, and a strange thing begins to happen. Steve goes into E's rote introductory monologue, repeating it verbatim, as though it were a sacred litany. (Any Elvi worth his salt knows the "Poke Salad Annie" intro by heart, if not from hearing Elvis in person at

one of his more than a thousand concerts in the seventies—
and many Elvii didn't—then from learning it from the highly
popular concert video *Elvis: That's The Way It Is*.) Steve not
only knows all the words, he speaks them in a voice that suddenly sounds remarkably like the King. It's like ventriloquism.

The band cranks up the grumbling first verse, and now
Steve's whole physique seems to change. He grows taller and
leaner. His arms snap, his leg twitches. He wanders away from
the stage, his jumpsuit glistening bright in the follow spot, and
struts between the tables on the dance floor. You can feel a
spark charging the crowd, who has just endured four or five
listless, mediocre Elvii. The band picks up on the energy, feeds
it back to the crowd, who pumps it into Steve. He is transformed. Something fills him up, transfigures the paunchy dentist into some sexier, more powerful being. He's possessed. It's
like Vodun or Santeria: the spirit of a god descends and rides
him. After all those Elvii wandering in and out, Elvis has finally
entered the building.

■ ■ ■

Libertyland is the small and rather dilapidated amusement park
not far from downtown Memphis where Elvis spent some of
his happiest moments from his teen years up until a week
before he died. Throughout his career, he would often rent the
entire park, at a cost of $16,000 a night, for private use. A sign
at the entrance to a roller coaster reads:

The Zippin Pippin was Elvis Presley's favorite ride. The
'King' rented Libertyland August 8, 1977 from 1:15 A.M.
until 7 A.M. to entertain a group of about 10 guests.
Decked in blue jumpsuit with a black leather belt, huge
belt buckle with turquoise studs and gold chains, the
'King' rode the Zippin Pippin repeatedly during a two-
hour period. He lost his belt buckle on the ride that

morning, and it was found and returned the next day. Elvis' Libertyland rental became his last public appearance. He died August 16.

Elvii have been performing in Libertyland's small concert hall every day of Tribute Week. At a show by Elvi Joe Kent the bleachers are packed and the small hall is so crowded that it's tough to find space to kneel down on the dusty concrete floor in one aisle. Kent is one of the professional Elvii, an entertainer in it for the money, not for the greater glory of the King. He's slick and "puts on a good show," and if he never really gets the spirit, he's good enough at recreating Elvis to draw slow, deep tears from some of the women when he croons "Can't Help Falling in Love."

■ ■ ■

"Good Rockin' Tonight" is an annual concert thrown by Darwin Lamm and *Elvis International Forum*. It fills a tacky, low-ceilinged banquet room at the airport Best Western with about a thousand fans. I hear Cockney accents, Scottish, Quebecer, Dutch, something Scandinavian; there are Japanese faces in the crowd, little kids, ancient great-grandmas, numerous young couples in their twenties.

In an introductory address, the emcee dedicates the evening to Eddie Fadal, Elvis' friend from Waco, Texas, a major collector of Elvis memorabilia and lore after the King's death. Fadal has passed away within the last few months; the news has gone out through all the fan clubs, in all their fanzines, a major disciple has joined E in heaven, but "both of them are here tonight," the emcee says, and the crowd applauds warmly.

The star performer, Terry Mike Jeffrey, isn't an impersonator, but a forty-year-old country-rocker who's been singing Elvis songs since he was a kid growing up in Memphis. He doesn't imitate Elvis, but rather evokes him, and he does it brilliantly. Much deeper than just the look or the sound, it's the spirit he taps into.

He does an "Elvis Unplugged" set that's pure genius: he sounds so great and has such energy I find myself thinking what everyone around me would surely take as blasphemy: *This is how Elvis could have sounded in his thirties and forties if he'd had the will to tell the army and the Colonel and Hollywood to all fuck off and had just concentrated on what he did best.*

After every song, a woman seated behind me complains, "I wish he'd do the gospel songs," and "I wish he'd do the religious songs." Not much further into his set, telling the crowd, "I think Elvis had more soul than any white man in the world," Jeffrey obliges her. The crowd applauds very warmly.

Jeffrey and his band are joined by D. J. Fontana, Elvis' original drummer, and Charlie Hodge, Elvis' friend and duet crooner, and the Jordanaires, the white four-man gospel group who were his original backup singers—now all balding, graying, and in their sixties. Jeffrey launches into an upbeat version of "Don't Be Cruel," and those four old Jordanaires open their mouths and croon the "Oo-woo-oo" and "Bop-bop-bop" parts in beautiful, velvety four-part harmony, and it sounds so right, so gorgeous, that even for us who were never fans back then it's somehow like coming home, back to a place we've never been. A return to Zenda.

Between sets Sam Phillips himself comes out onstage to a standing ovation and preaches us a rousing gospel of rock 'n' roll, doing a whole evangelist thing on us, thundering lines like, "The spirit of Sun has gone around the world four hundred million times! And it's NEVER gonna stop! The sun NEVER set on Sun!" He'p me somebody.

"Good Rockin' Tonight" goes on for four hours. For his finale Jeffrey launches into the King's mighty "American Trilogy," a mountain of pop-operatic bombast that's part gospel hymn, part Elvis National Anthem. "American Trilogy" is K2 for Elvis impersonators, the ultimate test; of the dozens of impersonators I've seen, there is not one but was broken and dashed attempting to scale it.

The opening notes bring a deep hush to the crowd. I look around and see tears welling up in the audience's eyes. By the middle section it has gripped the entire crowd and lifted them to their feet. They're standing on their chairs, hands linked over their heads, swaying from side to side. *So hush little baby/Don't you cry/You know your daddy's bound to die/But all my trials Lord will soon be over.* As the song builds to its *Glory, glory hallelujah* finale—and Jeffrey nails it—ecstatic waves crash over the audience, rolling back and forth between him and them, and I feel my hair stand on end. It's white-people gospel church, Elvis' holy ghost descending on that ugly Best Western banquet room and filling it up with his spirit, transmogrifying it for just a moment into the heart of his worldwide Amazing Graceland. If you could focus the feeling in that room into a beam and shoot it over to the Meditation Garden, it would lift him from his grave. If in fact he's in there.

■ ■ ■

A *New York Times* reporter covering Tribute Week in 1987 noted that it "is no more a musical pilgrimage than a trip to the Vatican is an art appreciation tour." A year later, an Episcopalian minister in Mississippi told *Time* magazine, "This has the makings of the rise of a new religion. . . . Elvis is the god, and Graceland the shrine." After visiting Graceland with his students in 1992, Douglas Brinkley wrote in *Majic Bus* that "Graceland is truly a religious shrine, and Elvis is a religious movement. Long as the movement doesn't preach hate or injure anyone, what's the harm?"

Though Elvis' most devout followers take understandable care to avoid both blasphemy and ridicule, the religious overtones and trappings of Elvis Week are everywhere and unmistakable, if a bit unorganized and inchoate. They coalesce into full ceremony on the night of August 15, the eve of the King's passing.

It is a warm, dark night in Memphis at 9 P.M., and I'm standing halfway up the Graceland hill. A coquettish half-moon hangs high in the sky, cicadas are throbbing in the decorous trees, crickets ringing on the manicured lawn, camera crews from CNN and the networks are jockeying for sight lines on the curved driveway. Elvis' voice, softly singing the love songs and gospel tunes, drifts over us from speakers strategically placed all over the property. Graceland itself sits quietly on top of the hill, lit up by severe white spotlights that make it look less than quite real. It looks like a funeral home.

At the bottom of the drive Graceland's gate is wide open, but the entrance is blocked by sawhorses and a small army of uniformed private security. Next to the gate, on a flatbed truck parked just inside the stone wall, a grandmotherly representative of the Elvis Country Fan Club of Austin, Texas, speaks into a mic. "Will everyone please bow their head in silent prayer," she says.

Outside, lined up eight deep along the wall and spilling out in a mass across Elvis Presley Boulevard, a crowd I estimate at about ten thousand (other estimates make it twenty thousand) falls impressively silent for a moment; ten thousand bowed heads and sober faces softly haloed in the reddish glow of the long white candles they're holding. Behind them, Graceland Plaza is jazzy with neon and halogens. Cop cars flanking the road a few hundred yards in either direction whirl their red and blue lights. The white nose of E's jet the *Lisa Marie* pokes over a fence across the street, where it is parked next to the Elvis shopping mall.

"Amen."

Everyone looks up. This is what they've all come for, converging here from around the world: the Candlelight Vigil, the culmination of Elvis Week.

From behind me, two middle-aged men in Elvis Country t-shirts begin a formal procession down the driveway, carrying blazing lawn torches that are said to have been lit from the eternal flame in the Meditation Garden. Cameras trail them down to the gate. The crowd outside lifts ten thousand candles overhead. Swaying back and forth, they begin to sing along with Elvis, "Can't Help Falling in Love." The last song he ever sang in public, it has extraordinary significance to the fans. They sing it sweetly, the women far outsinging the men, whom they outnumber probably four to one. The world's biggest assembly of back-up singers, a chorus fit for the King.

The candlelight procession begins. The two guys with the lawn torches lead the way up the drive, self-conscious, setting a funereal pace, the network cameramen walking backwards ahead of them. One by one, the fans with their candles pass through the gate. A single-file trail of flickering lights and haloed faces snakes up the hill under the trees, as Elvis songs continue to waft across the lawn.

The hush, the solemnity, the guttering candles . . . there's a kind of grass-roots grandeur to it all that's reminiscent of populist Roman Catholicism—Day of the Dead celebrations in Mexico, say, or a procession of the Virgin in a small Italian town—with an Elvisian touch of Hawaiian/Tiki torchlit paganism.

The procession reaches the top of the hill and turns up the path toward the Meditation Garden. The path is lined with dozens of handmade wreaths and plastic floral displays sent or brought here by fans. They're shaped like guitars, like broken hearts, like Elvis' TCB lightning bolt, like the fans' home states or the flags of their home nations. They're adorned with likenesses of Elvis or with teddy bears. Most carry a message of love for him. ("We all thank you, Lord," the note on a small bouquet says, "for sending Elvis in our lives.") I see displays from France and Germany, from England and Switzerland, from Norway and Belgium and Japan, from Texas and Baltimore and Chicago and New Hampshire (the Granite State, "Solid as his rock"), and many other places. Graceland receives so many arrangements that they can't all be stored on the grounds; many that are not too specifically Elvis oriented are donated to local hospitals and senior centers. It's a gesture Elvis would have approved of.

With the tv crews, I walk ahead and pick a spot against the wall of the Meditation Garden. The fountain is blue lit and bubbling, with four flaming braziers at the compass points. A number of wreaths have been placed around the graves. The security guards are in the shadows again, radios crackling. The horses are watching over their fence.

The two guys with the lawn torches lead the procession in a slow circle around the graves. The Elvis Country ladies are first in line; I notice now that their candles are battery operated. Next comes a small group who call themselves the Gates of Graceland. They camped out by the wall last night, squatting there for twenty-four hours. Later I hear that one adolescent boy among them, exhausted, suffers an asthma attack and has to be taken off in an ambulance.

More fan clubs follow. Undeniably, they are mostly middle-aged women. Members of each club dress in identical uniforms, wear their hair in identical dos, even walk an identical walk. Watching them file past the grave in their uniform outfits—blue t-shirts and white slacks for this club, pink t-shirts and slacks for the next, and so on—it strikes me that if the Elvii are the priests of Elvis, these fan-club women are the different orders of nuns.

Now come the sick, the lame, the halt, in wheelchairs, on crutches, some with barely the strength to hold up their candles. Some weeping, murmuring what I believe are prayers; others with that slack, blank gaze of the very ill. One Elvi pushes his mother's wheelchair. In my notebook I write *American Lourdes,* knowing that it's hardly an original observation.

After the fan clubs comes the mass of regular folks. They circle the graves in good order, keep the line moving, head off back down the hill. These first in line waited hours and hours for this moment. It's over in about a minute. Humble, serious, some of the women are quietly crying. They wear football jerseys, shorts, Elvis t-shirts; some are dressed in homemade outfits of Elvis-patterned material from the shops across the street from Graceland. A few Elvii are sprinkled among them, though most are in civilian dress, out of respect for the evening's solemnity. A tall LBJ of a good ol' boy whips off his cowboy hat and holds it over his heart. A pretty, trashy young blonde has ELVIS appliquéd across the butt of her short shorts. There is a quintet of young Japanese girls, and I spot those Eastern European Elvii I saw during the tour.

Along with their candles, most folks bring flowers to place on the graves—red roses or blue carnations mostly. Thursday night there were some few dozens of these around the graves. Now, after the long weekend of visits, Elvis' grave has completely disappeared under a huge mound of them. Veterans quietly point out to disappointed newcomers where it is under all those roses.

A tiny kid, maybe four, is gaping at the graves. He lets his candle droop and almost sets the back of his older brother's t-shirt on fire. A goofy-looking little guy, balding, who looks like he might be a furniture salesman, is crying so much he has to stand out of the line. Face bent over his candle, he is weeping and weeping, wiping his eyes. Finally a companion notices him, breaks out of line, and comes over to him. She shows him how to hold his candle lower. He wasn't crying from grief— he's got a mental disability and was holding the candle so close to his eyes it was making him tear.

I stand up there for ninety minutes or so and just watch the faces go by. Graceland people and several Elvis Week veterans had all told me the same thing: the crowds not only keep growing in number every year, they're getting younger and more diverse. I wanted to see this for myself.

It's quite obvious they were right. The fan-club ladies, the fifty- and sixty-somethings who've loved Elvis since the 1950s, who've been the keepers of the flame for forty years, whose cells around the world form the nuclei of his global following, are still very much in evidence, still very much set the tone and run the show. But at Elvis Week '94 they're a minority—I'd say not more than 10 percent. In the crowd that follows the fan clubs up the hill, the large majority are the next generation of Elvis fans—people in their thirties and twenties—and the teens and little children who are the next generation after that. Very few of them could ever possibly have seen Elvis live in concert; many of them were born after his death.

Elvis' fans are usually stereotyped as poor white trash, working class, mostly southern, hillbillies, fat, and uneducated trailer-park housewives, etc. This may have been true of his earliest fans, but as early as 1977, when the crowds rushed to Graceland on hearing of the King's death, reporters were startled by their diversity. Many of the older faces I see here tonight, the fan-club ladies and their husbands, do look the stereotyped part, but the leap to the younger generations explodes the stereotype. It's true they're almost all white folk, though the young Japanese and Latino faces form a significant presence. But they're young white folk from all over this country and Europe. And it's obvious they're from all over the map otherwise: young couples who look southern and poor, others who are clearly middle-class Yankees; long-haired college kids, a few skinheads, some hipsters, and many, many of the type I saw the first night, the ones who are just sort of regular looking, middle class, middle of the road, middle everything.

No doubt a lot of them are here just as tourists, just to see. But the fact remains they did make the pilgrimage, many coming great lengths and at great cost, and they're not gawking or scoffing—they made the effort of waiting in line for hours, they're respectful, they're participating in the ritual, and I see many who are clearly moved by the experience, maybe even in spite of themselves.

I think of a letter I read in *Elvis International Forum*:

My father and I have just returned from Elvis Week in Memphis. It was such a thrill to take part in it. My favorite part was the candlelight vigil. Even though my dad had driven all day to get there, and we were both dead on our feet, we still stood in line for two hours (we were lucky) with candle in hand. The love that generated from the huge crowd is undescribable. I usually feel out of place when I tell people I am a fan of Elvis', since I am 15 years old and "I'm not supposed to like old music." I get so angry at peoples' remarks. If only they could feel the love I do. But while in Memphis, I was so at home. For the first time I felt comfortable singing along with Elvis' voice in public. As I looked around, most of the fans were older than me. They can remember when Elvis was alive. I don't have any memories of him. . . . I have only known Elvis as being dead. I know he was alive at one time, but it seems only like a dream full of black and white pictures and poses. But the amazing thing is that my love for Elvis, even though I am too young to remember, is as true and strong as everyone else's. All those people feel the same way I do. That was Elvis' magic: he made everyone feel special. He helped me through lonely weekends when I felt lonely and out of place. I knew he would understand; he truly cared about people. I am sure he still helps people in his own special way. . . .

When Burton finally made it to Mecca and laid eyes on the Kaaba, he was not moved much more by the structure than he had been by the Prophet's tomb in Medina. "There were no giant fragments of hoar antiquity as in Egypt, no remains of graceful and harmonious beauty as in Greece and Italy, no barbarous gorgeousness as in the buildings of India. . . ." he notes. And yet he *was* deeply moved (to the extent that the rather hardened egoist could be moved) by the experience of being at that most holy of shrines *among the believers,* his fellow pilgrims.

I walk back down the hill. The candlelit line snakes all the way down to the gate. Outside, thousands more wait against the wall. It's after 11 P.M. I had been told it could take until 6:30 A.M. for all the people to file past the graves. It's obvious this is true.

Out on the boulevard and across the way at Graceland Plaza there is more of a festival atmosphere, an all-night street party with the cops at either end to keep the traffic out. All around there are clumps of high-school kids gawking, fratboys drinking beer, groups of Memphibians who've crossed the tracks out of plain curiosity, newspeople giving their reports under bright filming lights. A no-neck monster of a red-haired kid in a gold lamé Elvis suit is surrounded by foreign press. He says his name is something or other, "but my friends call me Elvis." Does he like Elvis? "I love him." Why? "Because he was a nice man. He was *genuous.*"

The true Elvists are easy to spot. They mingle with this crowd self-consciously, aware that they're a freak show. A group of four women—three of them middle aged and one a daughter—stand at attention along the curb, in identical fan-club outfits and hairdos, lit candles at their feet, red roses in their folded hands, just staring, staring at the house up the hill.

I fade off to my rental car at some point past midnight. Thousands are still lined up along the wall. The curious con-

tinue to drift in. Even from blocks away I can hear Elvis music
floating out through the still night.

■   ■   ■

Mommy, I saw Elvis.
    Did you.
    Yes, but he's gone.

A BRIEF LIFE OF ELVIS

> Before Elvis, there was nothing.
> *John Lennon*

LVIS' LIFE STORY has been told thousands of times, by historians, biographers, journalists, novelists, satirists, comic-book artists, disc jockeys, clerics, gossip-mongers, muckrakers, and virtually everyone who ever knew or met him, from his father and his wife to his hairdresser, maid, and nurse. In Memphis I found a book telling his entire life according to his astrological chart. *The Life and Cuisine of Elvis Presley* and *Are You Hungry Tonight?* lay it out by the foods he ate. Any reader of this book surely knows the significant peaks and valleys of his life at least as well as Jesus Christ's or JFK's.

When famous people die, we like to read their lives like novels, with all events consistently leading to dramatically satisfying conclusions. Most lives aren't lived that way, of course, and the telling of famous people's stories is usually a mélange of fact, myth, legend, and outright lies. This drives conscientious biographers and historians batty. In the introduction to his masterful *Last Train to Memphis*, biographer Peter Guralnick declares, "I wanted to tell a true story. I wanted to rescue Elvis

Presley from the dreary bondage of myth, from the oppressive aftershock of cultural significance."

My book is neither biography nor history, and I wouldn't say I find the myths and legends "dreary" at all. When dealing with a figure like Elvis, the historian who is compelled to separate the facts from all the rest of a life story is in danger of being reduced to a kind of intellectual cop. Some of them, including Guralnick, are great cops. But there's more to the life of someone like Elvis than a Joe Friday approach can glean. Like it or not, the life of Elvis has a life of its own. Guralnick probably knows that his exceptionally detailed factual research only enriches the myth.

Fortunately, Elvis' life and career fall rather conveniently into phases, which we can easily imagine as chapters or books in future scriptures, a church-approved *Life of Elvis.* The simplest version, and the one best known to those of casual interest, divides his career into three decades: the Rock 'n' Roll fifties, the Hollywood sixties, the King seventies. Pop-culture mavens Jane and Michael Stern delineate a full eight stages in their *Encyclopedia of Pop Culture,* moving from his birth through the stages of his life to his afterlife as an immortal icon (or *Dead Elvis,* as rock critic Greil Marcus dubbed him).

Quibbling over the exact stages of E's life will doubtlessly provide future Elvist liturgists many happy hours of doctrinal dispute. My own outline, emphasizing certain mythic and legendary high points, follows.

I. A CHILD IS BORN

On the night of January 8, 1935, twins are born in the dirt-poor sharecroppers' shack of Gladys and Vernon Presley in Tupelo, Mississippi. The first, Jesse Garon, is stillborn. The second, Elvis A(a)ron, is born healthy five minutes later.

Gladys herself contributed an early piece of Elvis apocrypha concerning Jesse Garon. She was convinced that the boys were identical, and that Elvis, as the second-born, therefore sprung from "the root of Jesse." In *Elvis People,* BBC religion writer Ted Harrison notes that this was "a direct reference to the biblical genealogy of Jesus, which traces him back to King David and his father Jesse."

The ghost of Jesse Garon would obsess Elvis his entire life. While the family still lived in Tupelo, he often visited his brother's tiny unmarked grave. Under Gladys' influence, Elvis entertained the fantasy that he had somehow absorbed his dead twin's spirit, so that he was living his life for both of them. This might explain the "duality" that observers have always seen in Elvis: that Elvis is both the good son and the bad influence, demonic and saintly, hero and villain, shy and outrageously flamboyant.

Elvis was also plagued with feelings of survivor's guilt over being the one who lived when his brother died. Some analysts believe that his long preoccupation with death, the afterlife, and the transmigration of souls all ultimately derived from his obsession with Jesse Garon.

Jesse Garon's stillbirth shows up in Elvis lore in other ways. According to one legend, Jesse Garon did not die but lived in secret, and when Elvis did not return from the army, Jesse took over his life; this would explain the strangely subdued, acquiescent Elvis who went off to Hollywood and obscurity in the sixties. In his sci-fi novel *Elvissey,* about a parallel-universe future in which the Church of Elvis not only thrives but is tantamount to the state religion, Jack Womack imagines an apostate sect, the Jesseans, who worship Elvis' twin as their messiah.

On seeing the tragic finale of Elvis' first film, *Love Me Tender,* Jesse Garon inevitably comes to mind. As Elvis dies, his ghostly twin image, looming large over a quintessential Hollywood-America landscape, miraculously appears to sing "Love me tender, love me true, never let me go. . . ."

Some true believers like to follow Gladys' lead in stretching parallels between Elvis' and Jesus' births. Both were born in extremely humble circumstances—Jesus in a stable, Elvis in a shack. Jesus' father was a poor carpenter, Elvis' a scantily employed laborer and general handyman. Like the Holy Family, the Presley Family was a threesome. Like the Holy Family, the Presley Family was forced to wander from town to town. The death of the Presleys' firstborn son brings to mind two biblical stories: the New Testament slaughter of the innocents that attended the birth of Jesus, and the Old Testament plague that killed the firstborn sons of Egypt and finally convinced the Pharaoh to release the Hebrews.

Vernon Presley also contributed significantly to the Elvis-Jesus childbirth legends with his story of the miraculous blue light. Years later, when his son was world famous, Vernon would declare that on the night Elvis was born he had stepped out on the porch and beheld a heavenly sky-blue light pouring down from the sky over Tupelo, like the star that shone over Bethlehem, bathing the blessed little Presley shack in its soothing blue radiance. Sky blue is revered as the principal symbolic color of Elvism—Elvis' color.

II. THE BOY KING

The boy Elvis is raised in utter poverty, first in various shanty neighborhoods in Tupelo and then, from age twelve, in cheap apartments and public housing in Memphis. The Presley Family is a tight, inwardly focused unit, reticent among strangers, slow to make friends outside immediate blood relations. (For virtually his entire life, even at the height of galactic superstardom, Elvis always lived under the same roof with his parents.)

Vernon bounces listlessly from one low-paying job to another. Gladys obsesses over her boy, showering enough love and interest on him for two sons. He is extremely devoted to her, a mama's boy; they are more like close friends than mother and son and communicate in their own secret baby talk. Years after they've both passed away, rumors of incest surface.

Vernon is a bit of an outsider in this family. Early on, Elvis dreams of being the family provider. He promises Gladys he will become a rich and famous movie star someday, buy his parents a house and Cadillacs. By the time he's a teenager driving a truck for Crown Electric, he has pretty much assumed the provider role. He brings the $40 a week he earns home to his father, who doles back a few dollars for gas and sodas. A life pattern is set. In a few years, when Elvis and his band are beginning to tour the southern country music circuit, he will wire most of his earnings to his parents with telegrams that begin "HI BABIES . . ." Throughout his music and movie career, Elvis makes the money, Vernon (mis)handles it.

Boy Elvis is excruciatingly shy and reserved, a loner, a perpetual outsider. He devours Captain America, Jr., comic books, from which he later derives his dyed jet-black hair. He calls himself Valentino. From early on he is deeply infatuated with black gospel music, easily accessible to him both in Tupelo and Memphis. His parents give him a guitar when he's eleven (in alternate lore, thirteen), and a local Assembly of God preacher gives him his first lessons. It's through music and his unusual looks that he begins to make his impression on the world. Other kids call him "Velvet Lips" and rough him up for his long hair and fancy "Negro" tastes. At ten he'd won a prize for singing (sans guitar) the mawkish ballad "Old Shep"; by high school he takes his guitar everywhere, gradually impressing the other kids with his singing.

III. YOUNG DIONYSUS

In 1953 eighteen-year-old Elvis sidles into the tiny Sun Records studio and pays $10 to record a song, another mawkish ballad, "My Happiness." Ostensibly it's a present for Gladys, but he clearly has another agenda: he spends the next year dropping by Sun often, hoping to catch Sam Phillips' ear or find a local band to join.

In July 1954 Sam Phillips invites him back to Sun to record the single "That's All Right (Mama)." It becomes an instant teen sensation in Memphis, then a regional hit, then enters the *Billboard* country charts. Over the next two years he and his pals tour all over the South and the Midwest, honing their chops, building momentum. Success does not come overnight. The cool reception at the Grand Ole Opry in 1955, for instance, will become fixed in Elvist lore as an early rebuke from the Sanhedrin of southern music. An audition for Arthur Godfrey's tv show in New York City that same year is also a legendary flop.

Still, from the very first live appearances it's clear that this boy is generating some totally new and awesome sort of energy. Everywhere they play the group draws crowds of excited, adoring, and sexually charged girls and women, with their boyfriends and husbands glowering and grumbling beside them. By 1955 the girls are rioting at virtually every show, literally tearing the boy's clothes off him; one young woman describes him as "just a great big beautiful hunk of forbidden fruit." Elvis takes his pick of these fans to his room after the show, often at the rate of two or three a night.

On the road, meanwhile, Elvis calls and baby-talks with Gladys two or three times a day, every day. A story often told from this period emphasizes their unique psychic bond. One night in Arkansas, driving hard from one gig to the next, the boys burn out Elvis' new pink Cadillac. They stand by the side of a lonely road and watch it completely destroyed by flames. As soon as he can get to a phone Elvis calls Gladys to let her know he's all right. It's as though he knew she'd know what had happened. And, the story goes, she did. Before the phone rings, she has woken up from a terrifying nightmare and tells Vernon she saw their boy in a burning car.

In 1956 twenty-one-year-old Elvis Presley, now signed to RCA and managed by genius carny-shyster "Colonel" Tom Parker, becomes a national, then international phenomenon. The era of the rock 'n' roll superstar begins, and the world will never be the same. Elvis sells staggering numbers of records, causes mass hysteria everywhere he goes, is denounced as a demonic force of evil by critics and clerics and city fathers, makes historic appearances on Ed Sullivan's show, fulfills his dream of making movies, dates starlets, spawns an industry of p. r. and merchandising centered entirely on his looks and his sound, unintentionally causes a total revision in the way popular culture is received and perceived, and buys his folks the Caddies and the houses he'd always promised them.

IV. DARKNESS FALLS

The year 1958, just two years after his supernova burst upon the world, is disastrous for Elvis. He is drafted into the army, bringing an abrupt apparent end to his career. King Pentheus has shackled Dionysus, and the fans are stunned. It is in the army, driving tanks for two years in West Germany, that he most likely gets his first, fatally attractive taste of drug use. (In alternate lore, he was already experimenting with drugs in high school.)

Then his beloved Gladys dies, on August 14, at age forty-two, of hepatitis complicated by habitual drinking. (In 1977 E will die on August 16, age forty-two, at least partly due to his own self-numbing habits.) At the funeral he falls on her casket, crying out, "I lived my whole life for you!" and sobbing, "Everything I have is gone." At Graceland, he orders that the windowpane she cracked as she fell dying never be repaired, and that none of her things ever be moved. (Some say that nothing in her room, in the private upstairs part of the house, has been changed to this day.)

Vernon remarries within two years, but Elvis shuns the wedding and speaks of stepmother Dee only as his father's wife. "I will treat you with respect and kindness," he tells her, "but I want you to remember three things. Number one: You will never replace my mother. Number two: Graceland is not your home. Number three: Don't ever exploit the Presley name." He moves them into a nearby house. Years later, when Vernon tells Elvis he plans to divorce Dee, Elvis gives her $100,000 to disappear. After his death, when Dee crops up in the tabloids telling scandalous tales, it only proves to his followers that he was right about her all along. She becomes the most demonized woman in Elvist lore after Priscilla.

Gladys' passing is a terrible blow from which, by all accounts, Elvis never recovers. Many believe the listlessness and lack of direction he seems to display for the rest of his career stem from this loss—that his need to please Gladys had always been the source of his will to succeed, maybe even his will to live, and certainly his happiness.

Those who prefer to think of Elvis only as the young rock 'n' roll Dionysus insist that to all intents and purposes everything ends at this point—that, as John Lennon put it, Elvis really died in 1958. According to this view, the sixties are entirely mired in Hollywood dreck, and the seventies are distinguished only by his long descent into bloated kitsch, drug abuse, and death.

Those who adhere to this view have to ignore that Elvis made some of his very finest rock and pop recordings during the early years of the Hollywood period, 1960-63, when he recorded "It's Now or Never," "Return to Sender," "Are You Lonesome Tonight?," "Can't Help Falling in Love," "Little Sister," "His Latest Flame," "She's Not You," "Good Luck Charm," "Devil in Disguise," and other classic tunes. They must also discount some of his great work circa 1969-72: "Suspi-cious Minds," "In the Ghetto," "Burning Love," "Cold Kentucky Rain," and "Moody Blue," for example. And finally they must also ignore, as many of his pop-rock fans are especially wont to do, his parallel career as a gospel singer, in which he really only matured in the sixties and seventies.

Still, there's no denying that the Elvis who returns to Graceland from his German tour of duty in 1960 is a changed man—subdued, apparently rudderless, often brooding, often preoccupied with matters of morbidity and spirituality.

He also returns with an underage concubine, army brat Priscilla Beaulieu, closing a bizarre deal with her parents by which she becomes his live-in girlfriend at Graceland, continues her education and . . . whatever. Though it's hardly new for celebrities to display a taste for teens, it is remarkable how little controversy the arrangement sparks. Elvis' female fans are envious but respectful of her. Not until seven years later does he finally make a respectable woman of her; meanwhile he makes her over into his ideal consort, his bubble-haired and kohl-eyed Nefertiti, Mississippi Queen. Away from Graceland, his one-night stands continue unabated; in their own bedroom, she will later report, his tastes lean toward kinky role playing.

V. THE DESCENT TO THE UNDERWORLD

If the fifties were Elvis' Dionysian period, the period 1960-68 is the era of his Orphic mysteries, his willful descent into the Hollywood Hades. Orpheus went to Hades out of his inconsolable grief over the loss of his wife. Did Elvis go in grief to fulfill his promise to his mother that he was going to be a movie star and make her happy?

Movies are the collective unconscious of global humanity, the dreams and fantasy images we project as a group inside the darkened cave of the cinema, a replica of the darkened cave inside our own skulls. Was Elvis' descent into this darkened fantasy realm a retreat to, or a probing of, his own unconscious?

He churns out twenty-seven films in the sixties. They begin as spectacles of kitsch and devolve quickly into awesome banality and stupendous inanity. Sadly, he actually *did* have a fairly natural acting ability and boatloads of charismatic screen presence, as is best seen in his more serious fifties films and even in spurts in the sixties dreck. Like his screen idols Marlon Brando and James Dean, with some training and some proper vehicles he actually could have been a contender. He was given neither; his limp acquiescence in his movie work is a critical tragedy in his career.

Fans of his music will always be tormented by this strangely fruitless period. What on earth could he have been thinking?

It's possible that he was thinking very little, that it was all the Colonel's idea, that Elvis was in a zombie state, his mind blunted by grief, his ambition derailed. Then again, it was not an unpleasant life. The money was good—as much as $3 million per picture—and the work was as easy as strolling onto the set and mumbling a few lines. Dreadful as they were, the movies sold reasonably well, and so did the soundtracks. They nicely bankrolled the aimless pastimes Elvis used for distraction—the orgies, cars, drugs, and general horseplay with the boys in his Memphis Mafia, who endlessly followed him from Graceland to Hollywood and back again.

Writing of the Hollywood years in *Goldmine,* the tabloid newsletter for record collectors, Elvis specialist Neal Umphred suggests that, "A hundred years from now, this will be viewed in the Church of Elvis as the necessary 'fall from grace' that preceded the 'resurrection.'"

As much as I appreciate a record collectors' price guide openly acknowledging the Church's future, Umphred doesn't seem to understand how *fond* the Elvis faithful are of his movies. Elvists may or may not know the movies are terrible, but their enjoyment of them has absolutely nothing to do with esthetics. They love the films for their endless mirror-image reproductions of Elvis. The movie Elvis is infinite and eternal, and best of all to the faithful, he looks happy. There's not a sad or downbeat moment in the great bulk of his sixties movies. He's always happy-go-lucky and devil-may-care, casual to the point of seeming his own effigy, infinitely sexy yet flawlessly polite. He looks healthy, clean-cut, and in his mid-to-late twenties, at the peak of his manly prowess. Both well mannered and mild mannered, the movie Elvis is the most approachable of all his avatars, the most huggable. The rebellious youngster of *Jailhouse Rock* has grown up; the slovenly, stumbling King of the seventies is not yet dreamed of. Where those younger and older Elvises are distant as gods, as remote as Dionysus and Lear, the false intimacy that movies promote makes this in-between Elvis the most personable; not a Tiger Man but a Teddy Bear, just Chad Gates (*Blue Hawaii*), Lucky Jackson (*Viva Las Vegas*), Mike McCoy (*Spinout*).

Film Comment contributor Howard Hampton sees Elvis movies as a "self-referential nirvana," "Paradise Elvis style," a "heaven of cheapjack spectacle." "The vapidity [of Elvis' movies] is unmediated by delusions of grandeur, and as such may contain a germ of mythic purity," he writes. "It's an alternate universe governed by sheer whim, untouched by any sense of an outside world."

Hampton names *Viva Las Vegas* as the ultimate Elvis movie. "In the convex mirrors that are Elvis Presley and Ann-Margret," he writes, "every American fantasy of innocence and lust, flawless beauty and easy money, good times and charmed lives, is refracted. . . . It's an American wet dream, but a platonic one: a mating dance so close you can taste it, so remote Elvis and Ann-Margret could be Easter Island statues gazing out blindly from the ruins of a vanished race. . . ."

Trying to assess what he calls "the allure" of the "deracinated" movie Elvis, Hampton contends that the movies' ultimate message, whispered in "the voice of obeisance," is one of defeat and conformism: "*if they can relegate me to this, if they can replace 'Mystery Train' with 'Do the Clam,' what chance has a nobody like you got?*"

While this no doubt is the message *Film Comment* critics get from Elvis' movies, the message Elvis' faithful hear is surely something closer to "Paradise Elvis style." When they speak of looking forward to joining Elvis in heaven, they're probably picturing something very like *Blue Hawaii* or *Fun in Acapulco*.

Other notable points of the sixties:

In 1964, under the mentorship of Larry Geller, his hairdresser and spiritual adviser, Elvis begins to indulge his latent interest in mysticism and the occult. He dips into everything from numerology to yoga to the transmigration of souls and ufology. He experiences mystical visions. He becomes convinced that he has the power to heal and the power to alter matter with his mind. He contemplates the possibility that he is one of the great prophets of history, a Christ, like Jesus. At the very least, he's convinced that God put him on earth with a special spiritual mission to fulfill.

On May 1, 1967, Elvis finally marries Priscilla, allegedly at the Colonel's insistence. Exactly nine months to the day later, Lisa Marie is born.

VI. RESURRECTION AND KINGSHIP

In 1968 at the age of thirty-three, Elvis resurrects himself in a single stroke, the tv show *The Singer Special,* named for the sewing machine manufacturer that sponsored it and known colloquially as "the '68 Comeback." He performs before a live audience for the first time in years, wearing tight black leather pants and doing rock 'n' roll again, and the show is a complete success. The Hollywood years are over. Orpheus has returned from Hades.

The next five years are a crescendo of triumphs. He records his best and best-selling music in years, including "Suspicious Minds" and "In the Ghetto." He opens at the International Hotel, the largest venue in Vegas, beginning years of sold-out engagements there. He goes back on tour and sells out everywhere. His 1973 tv special *Aloha from Hawaii,* the first live worldwide satellite broadcast in history, is seen by over *one billion* people. By this time he has ascended to his full Kingship, become more than a man, more than a pop star; he is a global icon, a superhuman figure of folklore and mythology. Everything about him expands to mythic proportions.

Tragically and melodramatically, the 1970s are also marked by difficult trials and sadness. Priscilla leaves him in 1972 for a karate instructor she'd met, ironically, through E's own interest in the sport. Enraged, he asks longtime companion and bodyguard Red West to take out a murder contract on the guy. After Priscilla divorces him, however, he is courteous to her and continues to dote on Lisa Marie, his "Little Buttonhead" or "Yssa," who spends a lot of time with him and his girlfriends at Graceland.

E's remaining years after 1973 seem a remorseless downhill slide. His drug use reaches heroic proportions. So do his eating binges, the entourage, the orgies, his wild spending sprees and lavish gift giving. Sleeping by day, reclusive and remote as Howard Hughes or the Queen of England, Elvis retreats from the world and increasingly lives in his fancies and fantasies.

Meanwhile the Colonel is working him to death. Elvis seems to be constantly on tour in the seventies; he performs a mighty 1,096 concerts over the course of the decade, every single one of which is sold out. The show becomes increasingly bombastic and grandiose. No longer a musical concert, it is an audience with the King, all spectacle and ritual.

In his last two years, his mind and his health failing, he is hospitalized several times for intestinal problems, shortness of breath, erratic pulse—and, not coincidentally, a pressing need to detox. Increasingly depressed and drug-addled, he soldiers on, dropping occasional hints publicly and privately that if death came soon he'd welcome it.

In July 1976 Vernon fires bodyguards Dave Hebler, Red West, and Sonny West. Hebler is a peripheral character, but Red's known Elvis since high school, and he and Sonny have been part of E's Memphis Mafia from the start. Feeling personally and financially abandoned, the trio collaborates with tabloid gossipmonger Steve Dunleavy to write an exposé, *Elvis: What Happened?* The book is published on August 1, 1977, and followed by a phalanx of scandalous excerpts and quotes in the media. The world is shocked to hear of E's drug use, his voracious and kinky sexual appetite, his temper tantrums, et al., all revealed for the first time.

Elvis is crushed. Among the Elvis faithful, Hebler and the Wests are anathematized. In Elvist lore Red and Sonny become E's Judases, and *Elvis: What Happened?* sits at the top of Elvism's list of banned books, along with Albert Goldman's scurrilous mudslinging and Priscilla's memoirs.

On August 16, 1977, at the age of forty-two, Elvis is found dead on his bathroom floor. He'd been on the toilet, reading a book called *The Scientific Search for the Face of Jesus,* about the Shroud of Turin. (Alternate legends maintain that he was reading either an astrological sex guide or a medical pamphlet on enemas, but the eyewitness reports solidly support the Shroud of Turin book, and this is the only version accepted by fans and followers.)

VII. GODHEAD

Like many gods before him, Elvis' final apotheosis can only be accomplished after he has departed the mortal plane. Although

"Elvis sightings" don't become media fodder for years, his apparitions begin to appear within a few weeks of his death. So do the miracles. Iconography depicting a saintly or godlike Elvis proliferates. Objects associated with him become highly prized sacred icons. On the first anniversary of his death, the fan clubs hold the first Candlelight Vigil; Elvis appears in a cloud overhead, looking down over them. In the next few years Graceland is established as a world pilgrimage site. Thousands of smaller and more personal shrines appear in homes and workplaces around the globe. The ranks of Elvis impersonators swell.

After a few years outsiders are shocked and amazed to see that Elvis' following has by no means faded but has only grown larger and more devout. By 1987, the tenth anniversary of his death, it is clear that Elvism is a phenomenon that will not disappear any time soon. References to Elvis' godhood become common; his devoted followers are increasingly acknowledged as some kind of new religious cult.

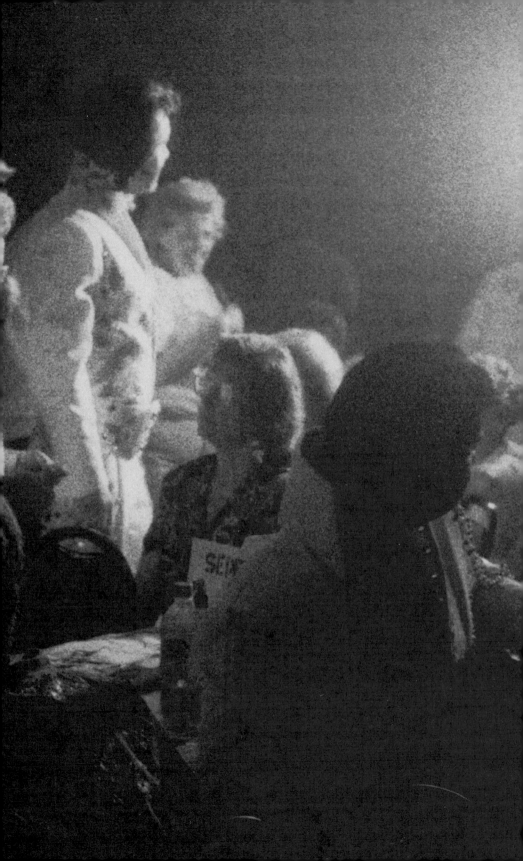

MYSTICAL ELVIS

Elvis Christ, Jesus Christ.
I went through the whole gamut . . .
Elvis Presley

LVIS MAY NOT have been a great religious scholar or leader, but he was in fact very religious, and he did come to view his role performing on the world's stage as a religious mission. If he left no great spiritual dissertations and elucidated no profound religious principles, he did leave a sizable amount of anecdotal material from which the faithful can build a figure of veneration.

Elvis was raised in the First Assembly of God church, a fundamentalist Pentecostal sect. He attended a church built by a great-uncle on his mother's side of the family. The services were typically filled with music, ecstatic experience, and speaking in tongues, and parishioners strongly believed that God can intercede directly in your life and work miracles for you if you're good and pray hard enough. The church also encouraged a certain limited independent mindedness in that there was little church bureaucracy; the preachers of this sect are ordinary men "called" to the vocation rather than ordained priests. They are elected in and out of the pulpit by the congregation.

Although Elvis never cared for what he saw as the hypocrisy and pomposity of "churchianity," he was a seriously religious person. Those who spent time with him, many of whom were nonreligious themselves, tell stories of how he often prayed, how he quoted Scripture, how upset he could get hearing the slightest blasphemy or sacrilegious word. In *Last Train to Memphis,* Peter Guralnick quotes Natalie Wood, who recalled that when he first came to Hollywood he was the most religious boy she'd ever met. "He felt he had been given this gift, this talent, by God. He didn't take it for granted. He thought it was something that he had to protect. He had to be nice to people. Otherwise, God would take it all back."

When he included in his historic "Ed Sullivan Show" appearance a genuinely respectful performance of the hymn "Peace in the Valley," cynics decried it as ploy to deflect the outcry against his provocative rock 'n' roll performances. But in fact, Elvis freely mixed gospel and rock in his concerts throughout his career. He harbored a lifelong, deep love of sacred and devotional music. The legend that the Presley family formed a popular gospel trio when Elvis was a child is apocryphal. However, it is true that a revival preacher was the adolescent Elvis' first guitar teacher, and his first public strumming was in the preacher's church services. He was especially moved by the uplifting spirit of black gospel music. Throughout his teen years he would often slip off to listen to the great black gospel preachers and choirs that abounded in Tupelo and Memphis, and to the end of his days gospel music remained one of his favorite musical genres—perhaps his most favorite.

Elvis' only three Grammy awards were for gospel and sacred music records: *How Great Thou Art* (both the LP and the single) and the LP *He Touched Me.* It's said that he worked harder on and took more personal interest in his gospel recordings than any but the earliest of his pop records. "Millions of people around the world are going to hear this album," hairdresser Larry Geller recalls him saying during the recording of *How Great Thou Art* in 1966. "It's going to touch people in ways we can't imagine. And I know this album is ordained by God Himself. This is God's message, and I'm His channel."

Among casual fans of his rock 'n' roll, E's religious recordings remain largely unknown; among rock and pop musicologists, they are underappreciated and disparaged. RCA marketed these records to a discrete religious-music audience, so although they always sold well, they never appeared on the pop charts, with the exception of a crossover like "Crying in the Chapel." But Elvis' true fans, like Elvis himself, make little distinction between his rock and his gospel, and the two are often played interchangeably at Elvist gatherings. If anything, devout fans are likely to say that while they *enjoy* Elvis' secular music, it's the religious songs that move them most.

∎   ∎   ∎

The foundation of Elvis' religiosity was basic southern Protestantism, but he clearly was open to many other spiritual influences from childhood on. Both Vernon and Gladys were superstitious and prone to premonitions and strange dreams. There are many stories, like Gladys' precognitive knowledge of the burned-up Cadillac, of Gladys' having the gift of second sight. Both she and Vernon were sleepwalkers and purportedly lucid dreamers, and they passed these traits on to their son.

When Elvis was a boy, Gladys apparently told him that one of her grandmothers had been secretly Jewish. Elvis later came to interpret this as a bond between himself and another famous Jewish son, Jesus. Through much of his career he wore two symbols around his neck, the Christian cross and the

Hebrew chai. He had a special wristwatch that flashed the two symbols.

It has sometimes been averred that Elvis' involvement in occultism and New Age mysticism was an effect of his drug-addled later years. But in fact it was in the mid-fifties, at the very start of his career, that a girlfriend in Biloxi gave him a copy of *The Prophet* by Kahlil Gibran. The book made a deep and lasting impression on him, and in the course of his life he gave away numerous copies to friends and acquaintances and would quote it as readily as he quoted the Bible.

It was Larry Geller who focused E's spiritual quest. They met in 1964. Geller, hairdresser to Hollywood's stars, had been introduced to occultism and mysticism by his parents, both liberal Jews. His father, who'd performed vaudeville with Borah Minnevitch's Harmonica Cats (which also spawned future screen star Lee J. Cobb), was a member of the Church of World Messianity, which combined Judeo-Christian mysticism with the Japanese healing tradition of johrei; his mother lent him her books of theosophical writings.

Geller says the first time he cut Elvis' hair, Elvis asked him, "Why was I plucked? . . . From millions and millions of lives, why me? Why was I picked out to be Elvis? I mean, there's gotta be a reason, a purpose, why I was chosen to be Elvis Presley."

Geller thought he knew the answer—or at least knew how to find it. For the next three years, he fed Elvis a constant stream of pseudo-occult and metaphysical writings: books popular among California hippies in the sixties like *The Tibetan Book of the Dead,* Paramanhansa Yogananda's *Autobiography of a Yogi, The Mystical Christ, Cheiro's Book of Numbers* (by "Count" Louis Harmon Cheiro, a famous numerologist to the stars), theosophical writings by Madame Blavatsky (whom Elvis liked because he thought she looked like Gladys), *The Rosicrucian Cosmo-Conception,* the UFO space brothers myths of *Urantia,* and *The Impersonal Life,* supposedly "channeled" straight from God by a mystic named Joseph Benner in the 1910s. The last of these was Elvis' favorite, and he gave away hundreds of copies to others before the Colonel and the boys put a stop to it. In all, Geller estimates that Elvis must have read a thousand books on spiritual topics by the time he died.

Years later, Joe Esposito, one of the highest ranking Memphis Mafiosi, recalled, "everything that had to do with the unknown was his thing. He always liked to know what was going on, and make up his own ideas. . . . ESP, outer space, etc."

Geller claims that Elvis adopted his famous high collars "because he was inspired by drawings of various spiritual masters wearing high collars in David Anreas' *Through the Eyes of the Masters,* a favorite book." In his book *"If I Can Dream": Elvis' Own Story* Geller reproduces a couple of these drawings of, evidently, nineteenth-century adepts looking romantically mystical, and you can certainly see how their tall collars may have been Elvis' models.

Geller introduced Elvis to meditation, which E called "the greatest tonic in the world." In 1965 Geller helped him design the famous Meditation Garden at Graceland. It was modeled somewhat after the grounds of Yogananda's Self-Realization ashram outside Los Angeles, where Geller had previously taken the actor Dennis Weaver. He took Elvis there in 1965. The King was moved and impressed by the spiritual teachers he met there, but he was unable to apply himself to the yogic discipline required of the students. When he asked his favorite yogi, the matronly Daya Mata, if she might show him shortcuts to spiritual happiness, she allegedly scolded him, telling him not even the richest man on earth, not even Elvis Presley, could buy an easy way to enlightenment.

When a young Elvis was first filling the airwaves, people joked that his name sounded like something from a science-fiction story. Considering the rest of his life and his afterlife, they were in a way right. With Geller, Elvis explored the spiritual significance of his name. *Elvis* is an anagram of *lives.* And *Presley* is said to be a southern corruption of the Welsh for *priestly.* Thus, *The Priest Lives.*

In most Semitic languages, *El* means "the supreme god." *Vis* means "power." So *El-Vis* is "power of God." *El* is the root of the Hebrew *Elohim* and survives in Hebrew names like Ely, Daniel, Samuel, and so on. In ancient Semitic mythologies, like the Sumerian myths narrated in thirteenth-century B.C. texts found in Ras Shamra (site of the ancient crossroads city Ungarit), El is the sun god, most often described as a gray-bearded god-the-father figure. But in one text, a mythopoeic poem called *Birth of the Gracious Gods,* he is a younger man who charms women with the size of his *membrum virilum.*

■ ■ ■

Memphis Mafia like to tell the story of the time they were driving out West. Elvis was telling the boys that he could move material objects by concentrating his mental powers. He said that they could do it too, but they needed to meditate and train for it. When the boys expressed doubt, he told them to stop the car. Getting out, he pointed to a cloud hanging motionless up in the sky. He stared at it a while and, well, it started to move. *See that?* he smiled with satisfaction. He also liked to demonstrate how he could make a leaf tremble by holding the palm of his hand near it.

Geller tells a similar story. In the mid-sixties Elvis was driving his tour bus through Hopi country in the Arizona desert when he was suddenly awestruck by a single cloud floating over the mountains. Geller described the incident:

"Do you see what I see?" Elvis asked in a whisper. I looked again. "That's Joseph Stalin's face up there!"

Try as I might to see it any other way, there was no denying that it was Stalin's face in the cloud.

"Why Stalin? Why Stalin?" Elvis asked, his voice breaking. "Of all people, what's he doin' up there?"

The cloud changed shape, becoming the face of Jesus, smiling down at Elvis. Elvis jerked the bus to the side of the road. He leaped out, Geller following, and stared in awe at the new shape the cloud had taken.

"It's God!" he cried. "It's God! It's love. God is love, Larry."

Tears streamed down his face as he hugged me tightly and said, "I love you. I love you.

"Oh, God is real. It's all true. I love God so much. I'm filled with Divine Love. . . ."

"Oh man," Elvis later sighed to Geller, "how do you possibly explain to a nonbeliever when you just had a vision? I mean, a vision when Almighty God touches you and reveals Himself? I saw the Christ and the Antichrist! Oh, Lord."

Elvis came to believe in reincarnation, but only for special souls on a path of spiritual evolution. He believed that he was such a soul, and that Gladys might have been as well. In fact, according to some sources, he believed that he actually met Gladys' reincarnation in the form of an elderly fan in the crowd outside Graceland's gate several years after Gladys' death. He was so taken with this stranger that he gave her a ring he'd given to Gladys back in the 1950s. He also saw Gladys' soul peeking out from the eyes of his last girlfriend, twenty-year-old Ginger Alden, and told Geller of powerful, prophetic-seeming dreams in which the images of Ginger and Gladys were indistinguishably fused.

Elvis believed that he, like Gladys before him, had special powers of second sight. Once, when Red and Sonny were singing Dave Hebler's praises to him, *Elvis: What Happened?* reports, "Elvis acted like he knew it all along. 'You underestimate my powers,' he told them. 'I knew what sort of man Dave Hebler was from the first day I met him. I can see these things before other people can.'" He impressed the boys and the Colonel enough with his intuitive powers that they became worried that Geller had somehow taught him some magical secret of mind reading.

Through the books Geller gave him, Elvis learned the occult lore (popularized by the theosophists and Aleister Crowley) of an eternal war for humanity's soul being fought between two powerful, shadowy groups of magi, the White Brotherhood and the Black Lodge. The latter are magi who've been seduced to the dark side. In popular superstition they are often confused with devils and demons; in the twentieth century their influence is most prominent in the perverse occult beliefs held by Hitler and various Nazi leaders. The White Brotherhood includes all the great spiritual masters of history, including Buddha and Jesus.

Elvis "didn't think Jesus was the only begotten son of God," Geller writes.

> He thought that all people had Christ in them and had the same potential. Knowing the Scriptures as well as he did, Elvis would pose questions like "Didn't Jesus say that you could do greater things?" Contrary to reports, Elvis' favorite book of the Bible was not the dramatic Revelation but the more mystical Book of John.
>
> Elvis' conception of Jesus Christ differed from the Jesus depicted by modern Christianity. Elvis felt that while on earth Christ revealed very deep, profound secrets, but that what we read today of what Jesus supposedly said is a watered-down version. He thought that Jesus experienced everything that all people experienced, that he was the

flower of humanity, that he suffered, and yet his suffering was ecstasy. Later in his life, whenever he felt that he was truly suffering, Elvis would say, "This is the way Jesus was. Did you ever see Jesus mentioned in the Bible laughing? Never. Not once does it say that Jesus smiled or laughed. That's because he had this compassion for other people. He knew where other people were at. He knew the sufferings of humanity. I understand that, and that's why I am who I am. That's why God put me on earth. That's part of my mission."

In the end, Elvis decided that he was not a Christ, not one of the "masters," but definitely a divine servant with a special mission on earth. "Now I know what my mission is," he told Geller reasonably, "and that's to uplift people, bring happiness into their lives. People are suffering everywhere, and it's only goin' to get worse. I'm not a preacher; I'm an entertainer, a singer. That's how God and the Brotherhood are helping and usin' me, that's my role, and I love it." Still, he always held out hope that there might be more. "And who knows? Maybe there's something else in store for me," Geller reports him saying. "Maybe God wants to use me in bigger ways. I feel it's so. I hope so."

At the height of his Christ complex, Elvis was in the habit of giving people a serious look and saying things like "I'm about my Father's business." When he was procrastinating over marrying Priscilla, he liked to point out that Jesus had never married, either. In one scene in the semidocumentary *This Is Elvis*, E is joking around with the boys at the International Hotel in Vegas hours before his ground-breaking 1969 comeback there. He's reading best-wishes postcards from Tom Jones, RCA Records, and the like. He opens one and pretends to read, "My God, My God, why have you forsaken me? Signed, the Pope." The boys all laugh, and he does too.

Throughout his mid-sixties three-year spiritual journey with Elvis, Geller was distrusted and disliked by virtually everyone else in the King's entourage. Although the King could sometimes spook them with a display of strange mental powers, the good ol' boys of the Memphis Mafia rejected the bulk of what Geller was teaching him as faggoty California weirdoism. They made crude jokes about Geller's Jewish heritage and his manhood. More ominously, the Colonel was profoundly concerned that Geller's hippie-dippy influence on "my boy," as he perpetually referred to Elvis, was distracting him from the serious business of making sappy movies, hit records, and giant piles of money. According to Geller, the Colonel actually suspected that Geller was using some kind of hoodoo evil eye to brainwash Elvis.

In 1967 the entourage of enemies succeeded in ejecting Geller from the fold. The Colonel, whose management had become somewhat distant and laissez-faire in the mid-sixties, roared back into control. He cut back on Mafia salaries and perks and warned that any of them—meaning Geller—who thought that his boy was "Jesus Christ who should wear robes and walk down the street helping people" should think again. Geller was soon out.

As usual, Elvis sheepishly gave in to the Colonel, though Geller implies that the war for the King's mind was not easily won. He insinuates that the Colonel literally had Elvis knocked upside the head, a blow that left him laid up in bed for a week, during which E's heavy use of zombifying downers and painkillers began. Geller implies that the Colonel played a role in getting his boy addicted to drugs to help insure his docility from then on.

Priscilla may have been more jealous and distrustful of Geller than any in E's circle. Geller says she despised him personally, constantly disparaged Elvis' newfound spiritual interests, and angrily rejected Elvis' many attempts to get her to try meditation or prayer. When Geller was no longer around, Priscilla made Elvis burn some of the books Geller had given him. Later she joined the Church of Scientology, as did Lisa Marie. At least some of corporate Graceland's cool resistance to any overtly religious expression by Elvis fans is surely a mark of her stewardship.

When Priscilla left him in 1972, Elvis reached out to Geller again, and they would continue their spiritual searching together on and off until E's death. With Priscilla out of the picture, the King more freely expressed his interest in the occult and mysticism, and his entourage, in turn, were more tolerant. The King would sometimes gather them all at his feet and have one of them stand up and read marked passages from books like *The Prophet* or *The Sacred Science of Numbers*. He was constantly preaching a New Age cocktail of beliefs to post-Priscilla girlfriends like Linda Thompson and Ginger Alden. On his last birthday in January 1977 he held a private session with all the wives and girlfriends in the Graceland entourage; for ninety minutes he delivered a spiritual dissertation and read them numerous passages from his favorite books, after which he handed each of them a $100 bill. "This is my birthday," Geller records him telling them, "and what makes me happy is not just receiving gifts, but giving. This is my gift to you."

■   ■   ■

There's much evidence that in his last year or so Elvis, like Jesus, foresaw his own suffering and death. It wasn't exactly miraculous: by the end of 1976 he was terrifyingly deteriorated, physically and mentally, and others saw death hovering over him too. Tabloid psychics predicted he would die in 1977.

Elvis spoke often, if confusedly, about getting his estate in order. He worried about what would become of little Lisa when he was gone. Geller records a nightmare Elvis had and described to him during his last months:

> In it, he and Lisa Marie are somewhere in the Holy Land following Armageddon. There's destruction everywhere, and they're traveling around in a large armoured vehicle, like a tank. Typically, Elvis' armoured vehicle is being driven by a chauffeur. Lisa begins crying.
>
> "Larry," Elvis said, "I look at her and I say, 'Don't worry, honey. Don't worry, honey. Nothing's going to happen to your daddy. There's always going to be an Elvis.'"

That summer, he told his backup singer and friend Kathy Westmoreland, "I know I look fat now, and I'll look terrible for my [projected CBS] tv special coming up. But I'll tell you this: I'll look good in my casket."

Meanwhile he worried about the legacy he was leaving to the world. After one concert he turned to Geller and said, "Now they have something to remember me by."

At one of his very last shows, in June of '77, just two months before he died, he muttered five enigmatic, oracular words that many believers would come to take as a coded farewell. "I am," he mumbled, "and I was . . ." And then he paused, murkily, and the show stumbled forward.

It's easy enough to surmise what Elvis meant. He was introducing the song "Are You Lonesome Tonight?" when he muttered that famous phrase; all he meant, probably, was "I am (lonesome) and I was (lonesome)."

This being rather too pathetic, in Elvist lore the context of the statement has disappeared, leaving only a shimmering, prophetic oracle I AM, AND I WAS. Was Elvis trying to explain reincarnation to them? I am, and I was, *and I will be again?*

Then again, Elvis may have been muddily citing scripture. In the Old Testament the phrase "I Am" (*eigo eimi*) appears several times as a statement of divinity. Elvis might well have been familiar with this use. It also appears in the New Testament, in the so-called Little Apocalypse passage of the synoptic gospels, when Jesus warns the apostles that many false Christs "will come in my name saying 'I am'" to lead the faithful astray. Elvis would have known of this passage as well. Could he have been trying to warn his followers against false . . . *Elvises?*

There's also a possible occult interpretation of these words that I've never seen cited in Elvist lore. I AM is the name of a mystical organization well known to occultists. AIWASS or Aiwaz is the name of a spirit entity who appeared to Aleister Crowley in Cairo in 1904 and dictated one of his most important books to him. I AM has Black Lodge overtones; AIWASS is a member of the White Brotherhood.

Elvis would have been aware of them from his readings. At the time of this concert Elvis told Geller, "There's a war going on. I mean, behind the scenes it's a spiritual war of light versus the darkness, and I'm proud to be a part of it." This is straight out of White Brotherhood–Black Lodge lore. Could he have been thinking of this great battle as he muttered onstage?

SEX, GODS, AND ROCK 'N' ROLL

In the skies above we know there is love.
We hear Elvis singing to Mama and Daddy softly and sweetly.
Happy is our king, listen to him sing.
Way up so high we know Elvis is rocking the sky.
And on a clear night when the sky is bright,
look up to the stars twinkling—for Elvis is winking.

Megan Murphy

CALLING SEXY ROCK STARS "Dionysian" has become almost reflex among critics, but Elvis was the first rock star described as such. In many ways Dionysus truly is a striking Elvisian archetype.

To the Greeks, Dionysus represented the uncontrollable, irrational forces of the unconscious, from orgiastic sexuality to animal savagery. He was the god of ecstasy, frenzy, wild abandon, and unchecked violence. Dionysus commanded the powers of sex and death, male and female, overweening joy and blind rage. His dual nature was signaled at his birth, a miraculous cataclysm of procreative and destructive violence, when Zeus struck the mortal Semele's womb with his lightning bolt, killing her and hurling Dionysus prematurely into the world.

Zeus took the baby and stitched him up in his own thigh, later "giving birth" to him at the proper time. Thus he carries the appellation "twice born." As a young man-god Dionysus boldly traveled to the underworld to find and rescue his mother, making her one of the Olympians just before he forced his way into Olympus himself.

He was always a stranger among the gods of the Greeks, an outsider from the mysterious East who burst upon the orderly Greek world with his alien music and licentious dances, sweeping off all the women in wild revels of evangelical fervor. He was the last god to enter Olympus and was a force of modernity and change; as such he met with great resistance from the established authorities, both on Olympus and on earth.

He was feared and hated most for his liberating influence on women. When Dionysus blew into town with his intoxicating songs and hip-shaking dances, the women were seduced out of all bonds of everyday decorum; they abandoned their husbands and children, rebelled against their fathers and patriarchal rulers, and danced off into the hills to join his orgiastic revels. He was the ultimate rival suitor, roaring into town with his gang of raunchy Sileni, randy satyrs, and Priapus himself. When Dionysus and his companions came to town, his bacchantes abandoned all modesty, acted as though mad, as though drunk or drugged. They laughed and howled uncontrollably, writhed and shook with libidinous passion. At the peak of frenzy they lost all semblance of rational civility and gave themselves up to savage violence. Any animal that strayed into their clutches was torn limb from limb; any man who attempted to control them, even their own husbands or sons, was literally ripped to pieces.

Euripides' *Bacchae* tells the story of this sexy new religion arriving in Thebes from the East; above all, *The Bacchae* is a cautionary tale about the consequences of uptight patriarchal authorities unwisely trying to bottle up the passions this new god evokes.

"Shake, shake, soon the whole land will shake, shake and dance!" the bacchantes sing. "Their feet ecstatic, the air vibrating, *Evohi!*"

(Elvohi?)

"As he shakes his delicate tresses in the tender wind, swirling—*Evohi!*—calling on them: 'On, Bacchae, on Bacchae . . . thump your thunderous drums, thump your thunderous drums!' "

The disapproving King Pentheus broods:

> *I have also heard a stranger has arrived,*
> *A magician from Lydia, fair haired,*
> *A wine-red glow on his face and lips,*
> *The grace of Aphrodite in his eyes,*
> *A charmer, yes. And he manages to be*
> *With our girls, day and night, enticing*
> *Them into the secret joys of this mysterious cult.*
> *If only I ever catch him and bring him*
> *Here . . . I will stop*
> *That hair-tossing, those curls perfuming*
> *The winds . . .*

He orders his guards to "scour the town for this effeminate stranger, stalk me this girl-faced thing who introduces this new disease to women."

When Dionysus is brought before him, Pentheus muses:

> *The figure is seductive, I admit—*
> *I mean to women, stranger, no doubt*
> *What you are here for.*
> *And not exactly*
> *A wrestler—not with those long curls flowing*
> *Down the line of the neck, inviting desire.*
> *The skin is fair—you take great care of your*

Complexion. Far from the arrows of the sun, you hunt
In shadows the body's pleasure with that beauty.

What happens when Pentheus tries to interrupt the bacchantes' festivities and restrain them from their ecstatic worship? They rip him apart. They literally tear his head off.

Elvis' Dionysian aspects are undeniable. Elvis burst onto the stage as a mysterious and dangerous outsider from an unknown and more primitive part of the world—let the South stand for the East. As was true of Dionysus, Elvis' birth was also an occasion of tragic death—and although there was no lightning bolt in his birth, it would later become an important symbol for him. As the twin who survived when Jesse Garon died, in a sense Elvis could be said to have been "twice born."

Like Dionysus, Elvis was a sexually ambivalent charmer, both male and female, fair skinned, hair-tossing, his figure seductive, and so on. Elvis goes crazy with the music, gets all shook up, evokes hysteria in his bacchantes, makes "mad" faces, twitches and flails "like one possessed." Like Dionysus, he made simple, single-minded and insistent demands of his bacchantes—"Love Me"/"Too Much," "Love Me Tender" for "One Night," give me "A Big Hunk o' Love" and don't say "Don't," "Surrender" because "It's Now or Never," "I Need Your Love Tonight," "I Want You, I Need You, I Love You," and I want you to "Wear My Ring Around Your Neck." But the relationship between Elvis and his followers had a dark, petulant side, a hint of potential trouble, a demand for a testament of devotion on the bacchantes' part ("Little Sister," "She's Not You," "Hard Headed Woman," "Devil in Disguise," "His Latest Flame," "Don't Be Cruel," "Stuck on You").

The ecstatic abandon to which Elvis drove his female fans is legendary. "It was wild, wild in the early days," Vernon once recalled. "I have seen his clothes completely tore off, his shoes gone, just scratched all over, bleeding. Just wild fans."

In Peter Guralnick's *Last Train to Memphis,* Mae Axton, co-writer of "Heartbreak Hotel," recalls being backstage in the Gator Bowl locker room after a 1955 concert. "I heard feet like a thundering herd, and the next thing I knew I heard this voice from the shower area. I started running, and three or four policemen started running, too, and by the time we got there several hundred [girls] must have crawled in—well, maybe not that many, but a lot—and Elvis was on top of one of the showers looking sheepish and scared, like "What'd I do?" and his shirt was shredded and his coat was torn to pieces. Somebody had even gotten his belt and his socks and these cute little boots—they were not cowboy boots, he was up there with nothing but his pants on and they were trying to pull at *them* up on the shower."

In *Elvis: What Happened?,* Red West recalls many similar scenes of frenzied fans "trying to eat him all up. They were tearing and clawing like animals. . . . It was just scary for me to see what human beings could be driven to. . . . There was madness out there. . . ."

This Is Elvis quotes Elvis remembering, "Wherever we went, people wanted to get to us. They didn't try to hurt me or anything. They just wanted to take a part of me home as a souvenir, that's all."

Red describes what became of the patriarchal authorities when they tried to restrain Elvis' bacchantes. He remembers that at one concert thirty police officers guarding the stage were overrun by frenzied women. "Those cops were getting badly hurt. . . . They just crushed these guys against the stage. Knocked the hell out of them. They pulled Charlie Hodge off the stage and passed him over their heads like baggage. When they decided he was too small a fish, they threw him back like a javelin."

"People in these crowds aren't people any more," Sonny West adds. "They become absolute animals. They are ordinary honest men and housewives and stuff and yet when they get in that crowd when Elvis is up there, they become wild, wild animals." Even the Catholic newspaper *America* reported in the 1950s that "The youngsters at the shows . . . literally 'went wild,' some of them actually rolling in the aisles."

Red once saw something reminiscent of the Greek bacchantes yanking Pentheus' head off: one of Elvis' scarves looped around a fan's neck, "and a pair of maniacs grabbed both ends. Well, they would not let go. This girl is choking to death and the sons of bitches would not let go. I see it and the girl is going down. She is dying, man."

Elvis clearly had a sexually liberating effect on his female fans. He personally sexually "liberated" hundreds of women during his career. The Memphis Mafia tell numerous stories of his voracious sexual appetite, of the otherwise "good" girls throwing themselves into bed with him at every concert stop during his many touring years, sometimes up to three a day. Red, Sonny, and the others, playing the role of his Sileni and satyrs, enjoyed the overflow. Husbands and boyfriends who stood in the way of their revels may not have had their heads torn off, but there were many stories, and a few lawsuits, about Red and Sonny roughing them up.

In more general terms some feminist fans believe that Elvis had a liberating influence on 1950s womanhood as a whole. Some go so far as to assert that without the influence of Elvis and rock 'n' roll in the fifties and sixties, there may never have been a women's movement in the seventies. Amid the stultifying conformist tendencies of the puritanical fifties, Elvis made it acceptable for young women to express their sexuality openly. Thus freed, they went further in speaking up for themselves in other areas of their lives as well.

■   ■   ■

Orpheus, the legendary figure associated with music and death, was from Thrace, where much of Dionysus' story is told. From what's known of the Orphic mystery cults, they were probably closely aligned with those of Dionysus. Some scholars have suspected that Orpheus was an historical figure, perhaps a Thracian king, though there's no real evidence.

According to legend, Orpheus was the most musically gifted man in the world, but his was a gentle, soothing music— Elvis in "Love Me Tender" mode. He was also a mystic with a dark, chthonic side; when he sailed with Jason he persauded the Argonauts to be initiated into the cult of the Cabeiri, powerful and extremely dangerous demons.

In Orpheus' most famous adventure he descends to the underworld to bring his wife, Eurydice, back to the world of the living. Failing, he becomes inconsolable over his loss. Various legends tell how he died. According to one story he surrounded himself with a coterie of young men, all initiated into his mystery cult, causing the women of Thrace, who were barred from this charmed circle, to become envious and enraged. They sneaked into the men's camp and massacred them all, including Orpheus. In another version he is also killed by the jealous women of Thrace, but this time they rip him apart, like Pentheus among the bacchantes, because in grieving over Eurydice he refuses to love any of them.

One thinks of Elvis' inconsolable grief first over the loss of Gladys, and later over Priscilla when she divorced him. The void these women left could not be filled by any of his girlfriends or sex partners. Maybe there *was* a conspiracy behind his death after all. Could one or some of his last girlfriends have played the Thracian women's part? Was he poisoned, maybe?

■ ■ ■

The history of ancient Greece and Rome is filled with examples of mortals becoming accepted as gods upon their death. Alexander the Great was worshipped as a god after he died, and in Imperial Rome great heroes and popular gladiators became the subjects of organized cult worship on their deaths. Of the sixty emperors ruling from Augustus until Constantine was converted to Christianity, thirty-six were officially declared divine (*divus*) when they died, as were some highly respected wives and family members. As apotheosized mortals these *divi* were considered a distinct subset of the eternal gods, the *dei*. But their divinity was not questioned. Temples were built to them and priesthoods were devoted to their worship.

The cynical picture Robert Graves painted in *I, Claudius* of apotheosis as a humdrum bureaucratic ritual only halfheartedly believed by the emperors and people of Rome has been challenged by historians. Some argue that, certainly through the Claudian period, Romans sincerely believed that their emperors' souls had ascended to the gods in the heavens. They scanned the skies for signs that the emperor had reached his destined place among the stars (like the famous comet that appeared after Julius Caesar's death), and they looked for omens predicting the current emperor's future divinity (as when lightning blasted the C off CAESAR on a statue of Augustus, leaving AESAR, the Etruscan word for *god*).

The most striking model for Elvis' deification is the story of the Emperor Hadrian and his young Greek lover, Antinous. Historian Royston Lambert provides a thorough account of Hadrian and Antinous in his book *Beloved and God,* and Marguerite Yourcenar's novel *The Memoirs of Hadrian* is also enlightening. Quite apart from all the emperors, athletes, and heroes who were deified in ancient Greece and Rome, Antinous offers an amazing paradigm for the deification of pop stars in the twentieth century. Unlike the others, Antinous became a god solely on the basis of his looks; only Antinous became a god because he was *pretty*.

The most immediate resemblance between young Antinous and the young Elvis is physical: they bear a startling facial and bodily similarity. Antinous' appearance is well known from the many statues made of him; what Roman sculptors lacked in esthetic flair they made up for with acute psychological insight and technical skill.

To imagine a statue of Antinous with a pompadour hairdo in place of Antinous' hanging ringlets is to look at an ancient Elvis. They share the same classical features: the thin, straight line of the nose; slightly hooded, brooding eyes; sultry pouting lips; puffy baby-fat cheeks that presage a tendency to stoutness in later life; long, self-indulgent locks. Although Elvis never exhibited the slightest hint of Antinous' homosexuality—if anything, he harbored a red-blooded paranoia of it—he possessed the same ambiguous polysexual appeal, a sensuous blend of male and female attributes.

Our concept of classic Roman good looks was in fact defined by Antinous. His image was reproduced thousands of times by the sculptors and craftsmen of late antiquity and served as a model for countless more statues "in the classical style" during the Renaissance and later classical revivals.

But Antinous and Elvis have much more than appearance in common.

Antinous, like Elvis, died young and pretty—younger, actually, and no doubt prettier. In A.D. 130, when he was between eighteen and twenty years old (the historical records are unclear), his handsome corpse was discovered on the banks of the Nile, near the small Egyptian town of Hir-wer. The cause of his death was and remains a controversial mystery. He may have been sacrificed, or sacrificed himself, to ensure his beloved emperor's continued health and long life. It was commonly believed in late imperial Rome that through such a sacrifice, one could transfer one's life force into another.

A more sordid possibility is that Antinous committed suicide out of despair, because he was maturing from a handsome boy into young manhood, and thus losing the emperor's love. Or he may have been murdered at the emperor's command, for the same reason.

Like Elvis, Antinous had risen from nowhere to glittering heights. He was born in a small backwater town, on the outskirts of provincial Greece in Asia Minor. His family was probably not as poor as Elvis', but neither was it distinguished. When a boy he was brought to Rome and trained as a page for the imperial court. There the handsome adolescent caught Hadrian's eye.

Hadrian brought the boy into his personal retinue and, it is believed, made him his lover. This was nothing unusual in imperial Rome. "Keeping a boy for sexual purposes was a minor sin for gentlemen of quality," historian Paul Veyne writes in *A History of Private Life*. "Brutus, Caesar's murderer, loved a boy so beautiful that reproductions of a sculpture of him could be seen everywhere. The lover of the terrible emperor Domitian and Antinous, Hadrian's celebrated lover, were praised by court poets. . . . Jealous wives refused to allow their husbands to kiss a beloved boy in their presence. Did husbands go further still when out of sight? By convention no one in good society asked such questions. The pet usually served his master as a squire or cupbearer, pouring his drink as Ganymede, Jupiter's boy lover, had done for the god."

During his few years as Hadrian's "pet," the young Antinous—not unlike the young Elvis—must have lived a fantasy beyond the wildest dreams of nearly any of his contemporaries. As the ruler of Rome, Hadrian ruled the known Western world; as his lover, Antinous was vaulted into a life of incredible luxury and indescribable power. Hadrian was a man of great complexity, brilliant yet insecure, an esthete and epicure who could nonetheless be brutal, a mystic attracted to Eastern occultism, and a restless intellect who traveled obsessively throughout the empire, partly out of curiosity, partly to escape the confines of decadent Rome. Life at his side must have been a fascinating adventure.

Antinous' fatal trip up the Nile culminated a long tour of the emperor's eastern lands. For Hadrian, the trip had a religious as well as political purpose. Hadrian was an ardent student of the exotic, including Hellenic mysticism and Egyptian magic. During the trip, he and his young lover were initiated into the awesome mysteries of the death-and-rebirth cult of Eleusis. There were magical overtones too to their trip up the Nile: as emperor, Hadrian was also Pharaoh, and as such he had the duty of traveling the Nile to ensure that abundant waters would reach their crops.

In times of drought Pharaoh's Nile trip would sometimes include a human sacrifice, a youth ritually drowned in the river as magical insurance. It's possible that Antinous sacrificially was drowned, or even drowned himself. His sacrifice would have been intended to ensure the continued health and prosperity not just of Egypt but of the entire empire and Hadrian.

This is how his followers chose to interpret his death, and the theme of self-sacrifice became a key feature of his cult. Antinous' believers dismissed the possibility that he was killed or killed himself because he'd grown too mature to be sexually attractive to Hadrian anymore. "The first sign of a mustache resulted in a major change in the life of a page," Veyne explains. "The pretext of ambiguous sexuality having been eliminated, it would have been scandalous to treat the now adult male as a passive sex object. The pet lamented the loss of his position. . . . Some stubborn masters kept their pets even after they had stopped growing . . . , but such behavior was considered reprehensible."

∎ ∎ ∎

On Antinous' death, Hadrian officially declared that Antinous had become a god. Within four years, the emperor had obliterated the little town of Hir-wer to construct Antinoopolis, an entire city dedicated to the youth's memory. Here he established his new religion dedicated to the new god. In *Beloved and God* Lambert writes:

People were soon flocking to his temples to hear the oracles pronounced by his newly established priesthood, to invoke his aid, his healing, his miracles and to participate in his "sacred nights," those ecstatic, uninhibited mysteries which were later to be castigated by pagans and Christians alike as disgraceful homosexual orgies. From far and near countless pilgrims came bearing offerings to Antinous: half a million jars containing them are said to have been discovered. The unknown young man had suddenly become world-famous, the inert corpse possessed of an immortal power.

Antinous had become a god, the last of the ancient world. His apotheosis startled those people used to the routine and tepid deifications of the imperial family. The necessary solemn sanction of the Senate in Rome does not seem to have been obtained for this swift ascent to Olympus. Unlike other mortals so elevated in the past, Antinous had a puzzling lack of qualifications for his promotion: no divine ancestry, no noble blood and, on the face of it, no heroic deeds. The informality was suspicious, and vicious Alexandria soon whispered that the apotheosis was no more than the whim of the boy's distraught and unbalanced imperial lover.

Nevertheless the deification proved remarkably popular and proceeded apace. . . . In the peculiar ecstatic atmosphere and religious climate of the 130s, particularly in the Greek-speaking world, the advent of the god Antinous was greeted with a spontaneous enthusiasm. . . .

Within ten years the cult of Antinous spread throughout the Roman world. Principle centers were clustered in Greece, in his homeland Asia Minor, in Egypt, where he died, and with some resistance, in Rome. He was also venerated from North Africa to the garrisons in Britain, throughout modern France, Germany, and Holland, from the Spanish peninsula east to the Black Sea, Syria, and Armenia. Temples large and small were erected in as many as seventy cities and towns. His followers crossed all lines of class and ethnic group, from the wealthy to laborers and slaves, from the largest urban centers to rural outposts.

In various localities, his myth was blended with aspects of favorite local deities and heroes. In Egypt and Greece, for example, he was assimilated with the older death-and-rebirth gods Osiris and Dionysus. When a new star appeared in the night sky, Lambert writes, it was instantly proclaimed "the eternally luminous soul of divine Antinous." His feast days were celebrated with joyous festivals "replete with choirs, hymns and elaborate solos sung or twanged by the resplendent gold-and-purple-clad citharode [priestly lyre-players]."

Antinous was not considered a major divinity; he was prayed to as a lesser god who could intercede on behalf of mortals with the older, more powerful deities. He was honored, Lambert says, as "a former mortal whose death and resurrection promised salvation to others. . . ." Priests of his cult ritually reenacted the mythic story of his sacrificial death, his descent into the underworld, and his triumphant resurrection to Olympus.

As would happen for Elvis almost two thousand years later, an entire industry celebrating Antinous' image arose. Antinous' beautiful likeness was struck on commemorative coins and medallions, which were worn, Lambert explains, "as talismans against evil or as tokens of salvation. The demand was so great in Alexandria, the second largest city in the world, that several official issues had to be made in good metal, then afterwards in much cheaper lead, and even then were so eagerly wanted that they were worth illicitly counterfeiting." Those who could afford them had collapsible busts of Antinous they could carry for veneration and protection when they traveled.

The sculpting of Antinous' features in thousands of statues, monuments, and reliefs was the impetus for the last flourishing of the plastic arts in the empire. Antinous was depicted as Pan, as Hermes, as Apollo, as a warrior, a hunter, a beautiful boy. Ludicrous as it might sound, one statue that depicts him as a Pharaoh looks uncannily like Elvis in *Harum Scarum*.

Villa Adriana, the massive estate near Tivoli where the embittered Hadrian reclusively spent his last years, was adorned with many fine statues of the young god. Soon after Hadrian died the statues were plundered, and over the centuries they were coveted by kings and popes and museums of antiquity.

As befits gods of death and resurrection, the disposition of Antinous' mortal remains is shrouded in mystery. Hadrian erected cenotaphs, obelisks, indeed, an entire city to his memory—but no tomb or physical remains have ever been satisfactorily identified. Hadrian may have buried Antinous at Antinoopolis, or he may have carried his remains or ashes to Villa Adriana.

In establishment and intellectual circles both pagan and Christian, the extraordinarily swift rise of the Antinous cult "provoked wonder and sniggers," Lambert writes. After Hadrian died in 138, detractors and skeptics expressed their scorn openly. Pagan cynics were accustomed to mortals being declared gods, but rarely had the premise seemed so scanty. It was one thing for emperors, great warriors, and great athletes to ascend to Olympus when they died, but that this newest god's only distinguishing achievement was having been the emperor's boyfriend shocked them. The youth's low-brow status probably disturbed them as much as or more than his homosexual relationship with the emperor.

Not surprisingly, the leading figures in the Christianity movement felt tremendously threatened by this upstart god and the challenge he presented. Christianity was, after all, still a struggling cult itself; it was only a century earlier that Jesus Christ had lived, sacrificed himself, and been resurrected. Suggestions of parallels between the lives of Antinous and Christ particularly incensed the Christians. A generation after

Hadrian, the pagan Celsus outraged Christians by asserting that since Antinous and Christ had both sacrificed their lives for others, the honor that Christians give to Jesus was no different from that paid to Hadrian's favorite. It must have also galled Christians to see representations of Antinous assimilating aspects of Osiris, Dionysus, and Hermes as had their very early representations of Christ.

The Christian ascetic Origen dismissed Antinous' divine powers as mere Egyptian magic and spells. Other Christian writers deplored the scandalous homosexuality that marked Antinous' life and the festivities of his followers. In Antinoopolis especially, music and theater feasts seem to have devolved into drunken homosexual orgies. Clement of Alexandria called them "really shameful," and Tertullian, the Christian polemicist, derided Antinous as a god of pederasts and buggers. Juvenal derisively described Antinous' followers as "slurred of speech and lurching from booze . . . all greasy with rank pomade. . . ."

These Christians were, however, perceived as an equally bizarre cult by their pagan contemporaries. Celsus, for instance, was shocked and disgusted that Origen, in a pious excess of bodily mortification, had castrated himself. Pagans like Celsus found such rejection of the body and its pleasures just as scandalous as the Christians found Antinous' homosexual orgies.

Some historians believe that the mass appeal of the Antinous cult peaked during Hadrian's last few years and abruptly dropped after his death. Lambert, however, shows evidence that belief in Antinous as a god survived among clusters of common folk for another two and a half centuries. Comments made by Antinous' detractors clearly indicate that at least part of his popularity stemmed, as did Elvis', from his sheer physical beauty. Not even his enemies—not the stout defenders of Roman machismo like Celsus, not even proto-Puritan Christian ascetics like St. Jerome—could deny it: Antinous was an extremely attractive young man whose likeness had an unusual power to charm.

But Antinous' appeal must have run deeper. Because he was a mortal—common, flawed, even sinful—who had, so his followers believed, risen to join the gods of Olympus through self-sacrifice, the common folk may have responded to Antinous with a warmth and tenderness they didn't feel for the older, more distant deities of the pagan pantheon. His human qualities, his passions and foibles, his joyful festivities, the promise he held out that any mortal may achieve immortality—all of this may have related more intimately to the spiritual needs of the common people than the dry, hollow rituals of, for instance, official Roman observance. Perhaps this intimacy explains why the belief in Antinous persisted for so long despite enmity from all sides. Antinous, like Elvis, was the sort of deity to whom common folk could speak with more familiarity than one like Jove (or his Eastern counterpart Jehovah).

Many of these qualities were attracting converts to the cult of Jesus Christ at the same time. Perhaps this is part of the reason why Christian leaders railed against the Antinous cult so bitterly. St. Athanasius was still fulminating against it as late as A.D. 350, and coins defiantly praising "Antinous the god" were struck as late as the 380s, evidence of a last grass-roots resistance to what was becoming the official state religion.

■　■　■

The resonance between the story of Antinous' rise to fame and Elvis' rise to near godhood rings clear. They bear a remarkable physical resemblance; they rose from humble beginnings to world fame; they were immersed in a cocktail of exotic mysticisms and magics; their deaths and burials were surrounded by mysteries; both mortals, they each underwent an instant apotheosis despite a "puzzling lack of qualifications"; a tenacious grass-roots following arose after they died and spread rapidly to a worldwide popular appeal despite establishment skepticism and scorn; the likenesses of each proliferated; each possessed a synchretic assimilation of other religions and gods, including the archetypal Dionysus, Osiris, and Christ; and both represented blatant sexuality and ecstaticism in rituals, including music and dance.

Late-twentieth-century America is not much like late imperial Rome. The late Roman world was crowded with gods and demigods, immortals and demons. The Romans added to their own pantheon of gods hundreds of deities from the many cultures they conquered. And each Roman god appeared in myriad variations. Pragmatic as it was profuse, the Roman pantheon included a specific deity for nearly every event and activity, from the most mundane of daily chores—one god to be invoked when plowing a field, another when going to the bathroom, and so on—to the most crucial rituals.

By contrast, the Western civilization that arose after the fall of Rome is staunchly monotheistic. Jews, Protestants, Catholics, and Moslems all believe in the same one god. Even the God atheists and secular humanists don't believe in, as Joseph Heller joked, is the same God. This God is lofty and distant and doesn't appear at one's side at every casual invocation. Inroads being made by other religions and systems of belief—by Buddhism and Hinduism, Santeria's polytheistic pantheon of saints, and various New Age paganisms and neoprimitivisms—have not significantly altered this monotheistic context.

It's small wonder that the notion of Elvis' godhood meets with such resistance. Our religious traditions, let alone our secular framework, have no precedent for welcoming a new god. Thus Elvists cloak their worship in syncretic Christian trappings and nonbelievers code it in arty hipster irony. And yet, despite all the denial, the basic pagan urge to immortalize and deify remains irresistible.

O U R
F L A M I N G   S T A R
O F   H O P E

With candle in hand, and tear in eye,
I ask myself why you had to die.
But then I remember you are not dead.
I now remember what the Bible said.
Though it is true that you are not on Earth,
you are with your heavenly father who gave you birth . . .

Kristi Row

THROUGHOUT HISTORY people have believed that their deceased hero figures will someday return to them as messiahs. The messiah of the Jews is the most well-known example; many secular folk heroes—and even a few secular folk villains—have also been invested with a messianic (or in the case of villains, antimessianic) aura: King Arthur, King Olaf of Norway, Alexander, Sir Francis Drake, the emperor Nero, Napoleon, Charlemagne, Frederick Barbarossa, and others were all expected to return one day.

Other purely secular leaders have co-opted messianic status to achieve their own political or social ends. Joan of Arc consciously exploited millenarian excitement to rouse the Catholic French against the Protestant English invaders. In the nineteenth century the Mahdi of the Sudan did the same to organize a rebellion of the Moslems against the British colonials. And Pontiac, the great Indian chief, used the messianic visions of the Delaware Prophet to incite his people against, yet again, the British colonials in America.

In *Salvation and Suicide* religious historian David Chidester writes that a shared experience of death is one of the great organizing impetuses at the base of religion:

> It has often been noted that religion arises in response to human limit situations, those liminal, or transitional, points in any human life cycle or in any human society. Ritual practices respond to the liminal stages of the human life cycle, the transitions of birth, adolescence, marriage, suffering, and death. . . . The ultimate human limit situation arises in the death of the person and the dissolution of the community. . . . The shared symbolization of death within a community reveals an essentially religious response to human limits that may not register explicitly in the organized institutions of religion. . . . This shared symbolization . . . reveals a type of invisible religion . . . in which religious symbolization may be diffused through the shared symbols, myths, and ritual practices of a community. These common symbolic forms are nowhere more clearly revealed than in collective responses to the crisis of death. It is at that moment that the most fundamental religious orientations and classifications of a community surface. . . .

On the Rays of the Blue Star
God sent you to this World,
To be the light of Heaven
To be the Soul's Rebirth.

Even as a young boy,
The Love inside you grew
And soon you were caring
For everyone you knew.

Lightning from within you
Touched the Soul of everyone
And little did they know
What the Spirit had begun.

Your Mother knew the Meaning
Of that Blue Star in the sky,
The path you were to follow,
The heights to which you'd fly.

. . . .

You shook the Mighty Heavens
With the longing of your sighs.
The angels were rejoicing
As they heard your Battle Cry.

The Holy Spirit moves now
To do the work He must
And begin the Final Chapter
For the Only One we trust.

As God is our witness
We know that you're Alive!
You are the Light of Heaven,
As the Phoenix you will rise!

. . . .

We follow in your Footsteps.
We try to sow the seed.

The Time is ripe for Harvest
To fill our every need.

We Watch now for the Blue Star
We Stand ready at the Gate
The Candles all are Lit now
Please don't make us wait!

We Watch now for the Blue Star
To shine its Light again
To gather us together
For the New World to Begin.

TERRINA RUSH

Elvis fans were as stunned at the news of his death in 1977 as other people had been at JFK's assassination years before. Just as many Americans are compelled to share their stories of where they were when they heard the shocking news that JFK had been shot, Elvis fans have a need to share their experiences of hearing that Elvis had died. In the early 1990s a Florida fan wrote to *Elvis International Forum:*

On August 16, 1977 my husband and kids were taking pictures in our new apartment before he and I went out to dinner. The six o'clock news was on and I heard the announcer saying that Elvis was found [dead]. . . .

My husband dropped to his knees and we stared at each other in complete disbelief. I started to cry thinking this can't be true, they made a mistake, it had to be someone else. My husband put his arms around me and we consoled each other.

My husband had loved, adored, and admired Elvis since 1956 and I became a fan in 1968. . . .

Those first months were painful for both of us. My

husband died in 1984 and I know he is in heaven with
Elvis. I will be there some day. It is unbelievable that 15
years have gone by and my love for Elvis has not dimin-
ished. On the contrary I love him today more than I ever
did. I miss him so much.

A fan in Maryland wrote:

I am 22 and have loved Elvis since I was eight. I never had
the pleasure of meeting him, but I feel as though I know
him as a person. I still remember the day he left us and
exactly what I was doing. I felt like a big part of my life
went and that I lost a great friend (still feel that way.) But
although he's gone, he's not! He's always there for me,
whenever I need him . . . He is a friend and everyone that
loves him and respects him as I do, knows that he cares
for us as much as we do him. I love you, my friend Elvis,
and I will forever.

And a fan in California wrote: "My dad used to look like
Elvis. I guess that's why I've always loved Elvis. Every little girl
thinks her dad is a king. But Elvis is the real one. . . .

"Most people remember where they were when JFK was
shot; I remember losing Elvis." She was eleven years old, and
when she heard the news, she remembers, "I had to go home,
because I couldn't stop crying. For the next two weeks all I did
was cry whenever I thought of Elvis. . . ."

In the 1984 documentary *Mondo Elvis,* Frankie "Buttons"
Horrocks, a fan well known for her fierce dedication to the
King, recalls, "I felt like I lost a member of my family. I felt a ter-
rific void in my life. You always thought of Elvis as living forever.
You just never figured that he'd die. A tremendous emptiness in
my heart." Frankie divorced her husband for love of Elvis and
moved from New Jersey to Memphis shortly after Elvis' death.

In Dr. Raymond A. Moody, Jr.'s, book *Elvis After Life,* a fan recalls,

> It nearly killed me when he died. My divorce had come through a month before and I was just beginning to cheer up. The way I heard about it wasn't the happiest circumstance, either. I was eating dinner in a bar and grill on my way home from work when it came on television. When the news came over the tube, the place fell into a hush. There were some groans and sobs. This one drunk guy sitting at the bar mumbled something about being glad that Elvis was gone, and three people were on him right away, calling him unprintable names. What a creep. I could have hit him myself and probably would have if those three other guys hadn't shoved him out of there fast. . . .
>
> Anyway, I cried about Elvis on and off for weeks. I still cry about it sometimes. I went to Memphis for the funeral. Loaded the kids in the car and drove all night to get there.

The day Elvis died people were already insisting they would never let his memory die. Instinctively they knew in that instant that they had to preserve his memory and pass it on to future generations. One woman came from Dallas to be at Graceland for the funeral and brought her thirteen-year-old daughter. "I brought her with me because I hoped she would catch some of the mood here," she told a newspaper reporter. "She's got to, because after tomorrow, there is no more Elvis. There is no more King. I want her to love him as I do."

Massive crowds gathered outside the gate at Graceland. Reporters were struck by the diversity of the people. One said: "They seemed to come from all ranks of society. There is no characteristic that set them apart. Some were well-dressed, others in work clothes. Some were obviously grief-stricken; for others there seemed to be something of the camaraderie of a wake. It was a classless crowd of all ages."

Reporting for the *New York Times,* Texas-born columnist Molly Ivins observed that "Mr. Presley's fans saw nothing to be ashamed of in glorifying in their sorrow. They were not offended by an instant commercialization of their grief, by the T-shirts reading 'Elvis Presley, In Memory, 1935-1977' that were on sale for $5 in front of Mr. Presley's mansion. . . . It is too easy to dismiss it as tasteless. It is not required that love be in impeccable taste."

It was the busiest day in history for the floral company FTD; over two thousand floral arrangements were shipped to Graceland, and when the grounds could hold no more, the rest were rerouted directly to the cemetery. This figure doesn't include the many handmade wreaths brought in person by fans themselves, which became the tradition. All told, an estimated *five tons* of flowers arrived in Memphis that week.

Outpourings of grief around the country and around the world dominated the media—which, paradoxically, were almost instantly struggling to downplay it all. Instinctively, as newspeople, and perhaps as middle-class intellectuals, reporters, and editorial writers, they found the public's reaction all too frivolous in comparison to the death of more significant figures like Martin Luther King, Jr., or the Kennedys. But the story of Elvis' death sold more papers than those deaths did, in cities around the nation. The Nielsen ratings were boosted for the two network evening news programs wise enough to lead with the story. The story flooded radio stations everywhere.

A columnist in the *Dallas Morning Star* chose to eulogize Elvis with a quote from Whitman:

> *O powerful western fallen star!*
> *O shades of night—O moody, tearful night!*
> *O great star disappeared. . . .*

. . .

Almost instantly, the grief Elvis' mourners were feeling turned to denial. Psychologically speaking, this is natural. In the early stages of grieving following the death of a loved one, psychologists say, the bereaved often experiences feelings of the departed's continued presence. The bereaved initiates a mental search for signs that deny the truth. In its milder forms this can entail brooding over memories and images of the departed, clinging to objects associated with them, or speaking of (and to) them as though they're still alive. In more extreme cases this can develop into auditory and visual hallucinations of the departed. This is often what happens with the suddenly widowed. As time passes and the bereaved learns to live with the loss, these symptoms fade. Elvis touched his followers so intimately that they have grieved his passing like the loss of a family member, and their mourning has encompassed all stages of death denial.

First, they denied that he had really died at all. Rumors of conspiracy and cover-up surrounding Elvis' death began as soon as he was—or wasn't—in the grave. Neither believers nor skeptics bought the official explanation that he'd died of hypertensive heart disease with coronary artery heart disease. To non-Elvists, the cause of death was clear: Elvis was merely another of rock's drug fatalities. Just two weeks earlier Red and Sonny's *Elvis: What Happened?* had been published and excerpted in the tabloids. In painful detail it described Elvis dosing himself with massive amounts of uppers and downers at least through the seventies. People who read that book found the coroner's evaluation an all too obvious cover-up.

Many of the faithful, however, simply could not accept the notion of the King as a dope addict—even in the face of the complete autopsy report being made public, revealing the alarming amount of drugs in his body when he died. Many of them entered a state of denial from which they have yet to emerge. ELVIS NEVER TOOK DRUGS, proclaims 1994 graffiti on the wall at Graceland. Some decided that the cause of death was *Elvis: What Happened?* itself, that the betrayal by two of his most trusted friends was what killed him. Elvis had died of a kind of heart ailment, all right: he died of a broken heart. Almost twenty years later, many followers consider it practically blasphemous to utter the book's mere title.

That Red and Sonny's book broke Elvis' heart is not, in fact, an outlandish idea. Elvis was distraught about it throughout the year Red and Sonny worked on it with Steve Dunleavy. He was dismayed and preoccupied with what the book would reveal. Toward the end of the book Sonny and Red gloatingly relate a desperate late-night telephone call Elvis made to Sonny, a last-hour effort to block the book's publication. Throughout his career, Elvis had taken great pains to keep his personal life and habits private; now this tell-all exposé by two of his closest disciples would destroy all that.

Some believers felt that neither the officially stated cause of death nor the idea his death was caused by drug overdose was correct, and they articulated several elaborate conspiracy theories to account for what happened to Elvis. By 1979 Geraldo Rivera was "exposing" the conspiracy case on national tv. Two theories that Elvis had faked his death emerged. One maintained that he hoaxed his death so that he could go underground as a federal drug agent. The other held that he did it simply to get out of the international spotlight so he could start a new, quiet, anonymous life.

Other followers did not doubt that Elvis had died, but they could not accept that he was "gone." They insisted and continue to insist that he is still present "in spirit." Ellie Mentz, wife of Elvis impersonator Artie Mentz, speaks for many fans when she says, "Elvis will always be there, no matter what. . . . It just seems like he's still with us, and he always will be. It's just really a supernatural thing. . . ."

The death denial surrounding Elvis has given rise to two distinct kinds of Elvis sighting narratives: Live Elvis and Spirit Elvis sightings. They're quite different from each other and serve very different functions in Elvis legend and mythology.

Live Elvis sightings do no more than to perpetuate the lore that Elvis is alive and well. In these Elvis is glimpsed fleetingly and is sometimes poorly photographed, rather like sightings of UFOs or Bigfoot. Spirit Elvis sightings, by contrast, have supernatural, religious, or mythopoeic overtones. In these Elvis' spirit acts in ways not unlike traditional ghosts, apparitions of the Virgin Mary, or angels.

The epicenter of Live Elvis sightings is, oddly, Kalamazoo, Michigan. Priscilla supposedly has family there who are connected with an abandoned motel where Elvis was believed by some to be hiding out. Within a week of his death, a Kalamazoo tv station reported that Elvis had been spotted walking alone up a lonely road. The real flood of sightings didn't begin, however, until 1988, when Louise Welling reported that she'd had several close encounters with Elvis over the years since the early eighties, the most publicized of which was when she saw him at a supermarket checkout in 1987. Reports of numerous other sightings in Kalamazoo quickly followed—at the Y, at a bookstore, at several fast-food burger joints. Town storekeepers began to tape "Elvis Shops Here" signs to their windows. The sightings occurred in other parts of Michigan too, including one in an East Lansing laundromat.

Over the next few years Elvis started popping up all over the place. He bought curios at a crafts fair in upstate New York, visited a Florida dentist, and was spied wandering around in a Syracuse, New York, trailer park. He was spotted on a supermarket parking lot in Wisconsin, in a convenience store in Mobile, Alabama, in a coffee shop in Ohio, a florist shop in Augusta, Georgia, a hotel lobby in Atlanta. He went to a carnival in Denton, Texas. He hitched a ride with a truck driver outside of Memphis, he was the passenger in a cab that cut a woman driver off on a downtown Dayton, Ohio, street. Two young women caught him laughing at his own effigy in a cheap wax museum in Lake George, New York. He bought jewelry. He went to the movies to see Madonna's *Truth or Dare*. He had hero sandwiches delivered to his motel room. Using the name "Sivle," he made calls to radio and tv talk shows around the country. He had a motorcycle accident and was photographed hobbling out of the hospital on crutches, one leg in a cast. He got remarried and a photographer was there to snap a furtive shot of the ceremony.

In Detroit, five young black men forming a group they called the Cool Notes were singing doo-wop on a street corner when a black, chauffeur-driven Lincoln pulled up. Elvis got out, sang a few songs with them as only he could, and returned to the car, which disappeared into the night. A driver in Texas got into a high-speed chase with this same black Lincoln and almost got himself arrested in the process. In a Louisiana bar Elvis got up on stage late one night and paid the band $500 to let him sing three songs with them. A small crowd of beer drinkers heard him do powerful renditions of "Jailhouse Rock," "Burnin' Love," and one number they say Elvis described as by "my old friend Roy Orbison" before he disappeared into the night, visibly exhausted by the brief performance. And at Graceland itself, a photographer made a Bigfoot-fuzzy snapshot of him standing in the doorway of the pool house.

Many of these sightings are said to have happened in the late seventies or early eighties, but the witnesses say they never found the courage to report them before Louise Welling led the way. Gail Brewer-Giorgio was the undisputed queen of Live Elvis sightings during their heyday in the late 1980s. In *Is Elvis Alive?* (1988) and subsequent books, she elaborated the theory that Elvis hoaxed his death and changed his identity so that he could go underground as a super-secret agent of the federal government's war on drugs. The various documentary proofs she cites range from the botched coroner's report to the controversial spelling of E's middle name on his grave marker. ("Aron"—probably an unintentional echo of Jesse Garon—is on his birth certificate; "Aaron" is on his grave. Brewer-Giorgio argued that this "wrong" spelling on the grave was a signal from E that he wasn't really in there. Music journalist and E fan Jessica Willis has suggested in conversation with me that this may be related to the Native American "spirit stitch"—a "mistake" intentionally woven into the pattern of a blanket or other type of cloth to avoid offending powerful spirits with the pretense that human craft can achieve godlike perfection. Elvis did, after all, believe he was part Indian, and the act would conform with his well-known humility.)

Brewer-Giorgio may have been the first to draw parallels with Hugh Schonfield's book *The Passover Plot,* which proposes that Jesus hoaxed his death. *Is Elvis Alive?* was packaged with "The Elvis Tape," a cassette of a telephone conversation with Elvis that was taped without his knowledge four years after his supposed death and burial. She wove herself into the mystery, speculating that her novel *Orion,* based on Elvis' life, had been suppressed as part of the conspiracy, and that an Elvis sound alike calling himself Orion was, in fact, Elvis, still alive, still singing, masterfully assuming the double-blind cover of an Elvis imitator.

■ ■ ■

The farthest fringes of the faked-death conspiracy theories are pretty bedraggled, but they are endearing. Fans know that for a time Elvis was much enamored of *Cheiro's Book of Numbers,* a numerology tract. They also know that in the seventies, when his concerts reached the peak of bombastic ritual, they opened with the regal fanfare of "Also Sprach Zarathustra"—which many Elvis fans recognize simply as the music from the movie *2001.*

Elvis died in the eighth month, on the sixteenth day, in the year 1977; 8 + 16 + 1977 = 2001. Or add his birth year (1935), his age when he died (forty-two), plus eight, plus sixteen: 2001 again. To diehard conspiracy theorists the meaning is clear. Elvis was leaving coded numerological clues that his death was a hoax and that he would return from his self-imposed exile in the year 2001, to usher in the new millennium.

"I believe everything happens for a reason," impersonator Artie Mentz says. That Elvis' dates add up to 2001, he believes, "is one of those mysteries we probably won't understand in our lifetime."

Elvis left his believers other signs that he knew he was going to be leaving them and that he timed his own departure. Gladys was forty-two when she died on August 14. Elvis was forty-two when he died on August 16.

During his last touring years Elvis sometimes brought his books of spiritual or mystical teachings onstage and read long excerpts from them, punctuated with his own rambling exegeses of their meaning. If for some it made for a terrible concert-going experience, for some of the faithful it was seen as the act of a holy man who knew his mission was coming to an end and was desperate to complete teaching his flock before he moved on.

I am, and I was . . .

"We don't know when God will return for the Judgment Day," reasons Jesco White, a West Virginian who has deeply bonded with Elvis' spirit. "That's just the same thing with Elvis. He will return."

Naturally, outsiders find the whole business of sightings and conspiracy theories absurd. Nonbelievers ridicule the ordinariness of the places where these sightings occur. Elvis in a laundromat? A supermarket? A coffee shop?

But where else would the people who make these reports spot him? These are the places where they live their lives. On another level, these familiar settings serve a purpose: their banality lends acceptability and plausibility to the sightings. Anthropologist Bronislaw Malinowski observed that everyday settings frequently appear in tales of the supernatural or the unusual. A completely ordinary setting not only makes an incredible tale seem a bit more credible, it also grounds an extraordinary event in familiar reality. *I know what you're thinking, but I tell you I saw Elvis (a space alien, a ghost, etc.). Right over at the Brite-Day Laundromat on Oak Street.* The very mundanity of the site gives a wild story a certain credibility.

Reports of unusual events often begin with a personal disclaimer by, or on behalf of, the witness. The witness is an average, everyday person to whom nothing out of the ordinary has ever happened before. Witnesses of Elvis apparitions (as well as ghosts, UFOs, the Virgin Mary, angels, and the like) are said to come from all walks of life. Often they are described as having no prior interest in the object of their sighting. This too lends their story more weight.

Hipsters and bourgeois intellectuals who dismiss the Elvis fake-death theories as tabloid superstition for trailer parkers meanwhile have an almost identical phenomenon within their own milieu—the Jim Morrison death cult. In many ways Morrison is a hipper, acceptable alternative-Elvis, another Dionysian god of sex, drugs, death, and rock 'n' roll, another dark, androgynous Orphic baritone who died a bloated self-sacrifice. In his rise to fame the Lizard King purposely crafted his mythological image as a chthonic phallic rock god, which to the objective observer is at least as tacky as anything associated with Elvis. Since Morrison died, the idolatry of his cult has included pilgrimages to his grave in France, a mini-industry of Doors imitator bands, and faux-biographical renderings like Oliver Stone's film *The Doors*, all of which match the Elvis cult in excess of zeal and lapses of taste.

Morrison's mysterious death and burial in 1971 prompted a tradition of conspiracy theories and sightings that actually predates the Live Elvis sighting phenomenon. The official report that Morrison had died of heart failure struck many people as a cover-up, as did the coroner's report of Elvis' death six years later. Rationalists believed Morrison simply overdosed on alcohol and drugs; his faithful followers believed the truth must be more sinister and possibly occult related. Some believed he'd been murdered by Vodun or witchcraft, both of which he was known to have dabbled in. Others refused to believe he'd died at all. Inconsistencies in the details of his funeral arrangements and burial were taken as signs that he'd hoaxed his demise. Numerous Morrison sightings were reported in the first two years after his death. He was spotted at a San Francisco bank, hanging out in Los Angeles gay bars, and in Louisiana. An *Orion*ish sound-alike album appeared, unsubtly entitled *Phantom's Divine Comedy*. (Years later Iggy Pop revealed himself to be the Morrison sound alike on the record.) There was even speculation that the CIA was involved in Morrison's hoaxed death.

Not surprisingly, the Elvis and Morrison conspiracy theories borrow motifs from Kennedy assassination conspiracy theories—as do the conspiracy theories surrounding the death of Marilyn Monroe. Though Morrison is an immortal of lesser stature than Elvis, JFK, or Marilyn, his death was met by many with a very similar process of denial.

■ ■ ■

Surveys of the Elvis faithful indicate that only a minority of them ever truly believed that he had not died. Reports of Live Elvis sightings peaked in the years following the tenth anniversary of his death, from 1988 into the early nineties, and they dropped off drastically after that. In the early nineties UFO abductions, apparitions of the Virgin Mary, and sightings of angels seemed to replace Elvis sightings in the news. If people continued to see Elvis, maybe they stopped reporting it to save themselves from public ridicule. It might be people just stopped *needing* to see him. Maybe, like bereaved widows, they finally overcame the stage of denial in the grieving process.

Spirit Elvis sightings elevate Elvis to a figure of myth and miracle, and tales of such sightings generally conform to the framework of folklore. Narratives of Spirit Elvis sightings often include elements of magic similar to tales by the Brothers Grimm. Many purposely convey moral instructions much the way biblical parables do. They seem destined to become sacred Elvist scripture.

Two intriguing books recording such narratives are *The Elvis Sightings* by Peter Eicher, published in 1993, and Moody's *Elvis After Life,* published in 1987.

These two books relate dozens of Elvis sighting tales; here are just a few:

- In the early 1990s, in the wilderness of the Florida Ever-
  glades, a young woman comes upon a tiny, secluded
  cabin. She lets herself in and examines its spartan,
  eremitic furnishings. Suddenly she hears a voice outside.
  The cabin's occupant has returned. She hides and witnesses Elvis himself, alone, singing a sad Civil War–era
  love ballad. She doesn't recognize the song, but the voice
  is unmistakable. Not wanting to intrude on Elvis' melancholy isolation, she withdraws but leaves him a note,
  telling him that she knows who he is and warning him
  that if he wants to preserve his solitude he should move
  to some more remote place, because others will surely
  stumble on his cabin as she has.

  A week later, she returns with a group of other young
  people. The cabin has vanished, as if by magic. The only
  trace of Elvis' presence is a message scratched very faintly
  into a nearby rock. "Thank You. Love EP."

- A troubled adolescent sits smoking a joint on the banks of the Mississippi, in the shadow of St. Louis' Gateway Arch. He is misunderstood at home, in trouble at school, a devotee of Satanic heavy-metal death music. All he desires in life is to be rich, buy a lot of pot, and screw a lot of girls.

  A tall, quiet stranger appears out of nowhere and approaches him. Identifying himself as John Burrows, he engages the reluctant boy in conversation. Over the course of several hours, including a walk to a nearby fast-food joint for burgers and sodas, he reveals his true identity. Using a Socratic question-and-answer methodology, he gently shows the boy the shallowness of his goals and the waywardness of his path. He teaches him to love his parents and have hope for the future. By the time the stranger walks off as quietly as he'd come, the boy has thrown away his last marijuana cigarette and vows never to smoke that stuff again.

- The son of a small-town Georgia policeman is hanging out with a rough crowd, smoking pot, drinking, generally getting into trouble. After a fight with his father, he leaves home without a word. His father is sure he's gone off to Los Angeles to try to get into the movies and follow in the footsteps of his idol—Elvis Presley.

  One night Elvis appears to the father in a dream. He takes him on a tour of a run-down neighborhood in L. A., shows him the very house where his son is staying. "Man, your son is on drugs," Elvis tells him. "You gotta get him some help." The father flies to L. A., which he'd never seen before except in that dream. He drives around town for several days before he recognizes the neighborhood and the house. His son is indeed there. "Dad, it's the funniest thing," the boy tells his father. "Two times since I've been out here I've had dreams about Elvis Presley. In both dreams he told me you would be coming to get me. He said he was worried about me. He said he would work it out." They are reconciled, and the boy returns home.

- A self-centered Yuppie, just coming out of a bitter and ruinous divorce, goes hiking alone on the Appalachian Trail in search of peace and some answers to the meaning of his meaningless lifestyle. He meets a fellow hiker, a tall, quiet man named . . . John Burrows. They camp together, share a fire and a meal. That night, under the stars, Burrows relates his philosophy, a mixture of Christianity and Buddhism, tough love and New Age mysticism. He gently guides the Yuppie to a reevaluation of his wasted life, his shallow values, and his lapsed religious convictions, leading him toward an understanding of the magnitude of God's works and the bottomless resources of God's mercy and love. They talk all night, and by the time the first hint of dawn touches a nearby mountain, the Yuppie has faith to move that mountain, and he literally sees the light.

  When he awakens later that day, the wise stranger has vanished. He has left a note, admitting that his name is not John Burrows, but he cannot reveal his true identity. He wishes the young man "the best, in your long struggle into the light."

  Days later, back home, he sees a tv show about Elvis Presley and learns that John Burrows was an alias he often used.

- A young man who likes to take risks behind the wheel drives his truck off a lonely Tennessee road. Down in a ravine, his leg broken, he confronts the fact that in that remote place he just might die. Then a tall, friendly stranger named John finds him. They struggle up the hill together. John puts him in the backseat of his car and drives him fifty miles to a hospital.

John visits his hospital room the next day. He pays the young man's $1000 hospital bill and vanishes, leaving a message scrawled on the young man's cast: *Slow down. Good luck, "John."*

- A black car pulls up at a dairy farm in Wisconsin. John, a tall, quiet stranger, buys a quart of fresh milk, which he says he hasn't tasted in years. He wanders around the farm, visibly moved by the peace and quiet. It's clear that he's running from something, that he carries some deep sadness in him.

  The farmer and his wife invite John to stay for supper. Moved by his quiet good manners and his aura of melancholy, they offer to board him. He pays five weeks' board in advance. That night, he takes the King James Bible to bed with him.

  After breakfast the next morning, one of the hired hands recognizes John's true identity. The farmer, astounded, goes up to John's room to speak to him. John has mysteriously vanished—bed made, car and bags gone. "Wherever he's gone," the farmer's kindly wife sighs, "I hope he finds someplace he can stay for a while, someplace to rest his heart. It's a long, lonesome road he's on. He may never get to the end of it."

Eicher cites no sources, identifies most of the characters by first name only, and offers almost nothing in the way of verifying context. It's impossible to know the source of his tales—whether his sources are at all credible or whether he has simply made it all up. In his book Moody has changed the names of his sources, but he does give much more information about dates and places.

But it is this very vagueness that enhances, rather than limits, the useability of such stories as Elvist miracle tales. Regardless of how these stories originated, the important thing is that they have been recorded for future scriptural use. Like all miracle stories, they're by definition vague and beyond empirical proof. They are a matter of faith.

Dr. Moody is a psychologist (Ph. D.), psychiatrist (M. D.), and best-selling writer. He has researched the gray area between science and belief, between psychology and psychic phenomenon; he has written books exploring near-death experiences and past-life regression as well as Elvis sightings.

Although some of Moody's research may seem like a college psychology department's version of creationism, on the other hand, his approach to the case histories in *Elvis After Life* is respectable and level-headed. Moody would probably like to believe that there's an afterlife from which the spirit of Elvis can reach out to his troubled fans. But as a psychiatrist he searches for more proximate causes of Elvis sightings—hallucinations, anxiety dreams, delirium tremens, and so on.

In ghostlore a distinction is made between bad ghosts and good spirits. Bad ghosts tend to be strangers to those who witness them. They come back from the beyond as agents of disorder and chaos. Good ghosts are the spirits of loved ones—spouses, children, other relatives, or friends who have passed away. They return to the realm of the living to nurture their loved ones, protect them from harm, warn them of imminent danger. American folklore also has a long tradition of ghosts who synthesize the two types: folklorists call them kindly stranger ghosts. They warn the living of impending danger, save them from mishaps, or point them in the direction of buried treasures.

With few exceptions, Spirit Elvis falls into the category of good ghost or kindly stranger ghost. The exceptions are certain poltergeistlike phenomena, reported by Moody and others, that are said to have occurred the day Elvis died in 1977. Fans found their Elvis records mysteriously melted, their framed portraits of him cracked; Elvis figurines leaped off mantelpieces and shattered. But in many religions, including Christianity, the death of a god is accompanied by strange physical and/or psychic disturbances.

Miracle cures are another popular motif in Spirit Elvis sightings. Among Elvis followers there are many tales of his appearing in dreams or visions to fans suffering physical ailments or emotional strife. Elvis' spirit brings them emotional succor and often cures or at least eases the pain of their arthritis, backache, and so on. Flora Haas, an elderly fan, reports that Elvis appears to her often. "Elvis is my therapy for depression, pain, frustration, whatever. I'm confined to my home since 1982 because of severe health problems and spend a lot of time with Elvis," she reports.

Among the miracle-cure tales is a distinct subgenre in which the recipients of E's restorative powers are children or young adults. Rather than through visions or dreams, Elvis reaches them through his music.

A typical story of this type is of a comatose child diagnosed as beyond the reach of medical science. A nurse or a cleaning person working in the child's room is listening to a transistor radio. An Elvis song comes on the radio and, miraculously, the child stirs. A tape recorder is set up by the bed, and Elvis tapes are broadcast nonstop to the unconscious child. Slowly, the power of Elvis' songs draws the child out of the coma, and a tearful embrace with the parents ensues as Elvis' voice croons softly in the background.

The child and/or parents might have been Elvis fans all along. But even stronger proof of Elvis' miracle powers are cases in which the child is said never to have heard or enjoyed his music before. Most remarkable of all are tales of a child under the bad influence of Satanic heavy-metal music until discovering the greater rewards to be reaped in Elvis' voice.

Dr. Moody tells the story of a couple who are Elvis fans who have a daughter afflicted with Down's syndrome and various physical complications. During her brief life, their daughter becomes a fan as well.

At the age of ten, the girl becomes mortally ill. On her deathbed she tells her parents not to be sad. In her final moment, the mother tells Moody,

> she seemed to light up. The light looked as though it were coming from within her. She smiled a big smile. . . . Then she said, "Here comes Elvis." She was looking upwards and holding her arms out like she was trying to reach toward someone and hug them. She said it twice, "Here comes Elvis." Then she collapsed and died. She had the most beautiful smile on her face as she died, like an angel. She saw Elvis when she died. How nice. Just like him, isn't it? He was always doing nice things for people while he was here with us, and I guess he is still doing nice things for people where he is now, too. He was there to meet our little retarded daughter when she died, and she let us see that she was going to go on living, too. Never again since that night have I had any fear of death. I'll always love Elvis for what he did for Jennifer.

Tales of Elvis effecting miracle cures from beyond the grave are lent more credence by stories of the living Elvis. He liked to practice healing by the laying on of hands on the Memphis Mafia, laying his healing hands on their bruised shoulders and twisted ankles after a rough game of touch football on the Graceland lawn. The boys have always said that the pain did not actually go away, but they often played along and pretended it did.

Sam Thompson, member of the Memphis Mafia and brother of E's girlfriend Linda Thompson, recounts an amusing story of a time when his wife was in a hospital maternity ward, having just given birth. Elvis and the boys decided in the middle of the night to go see the new baby. As they were parading down the hall, causing an uproar among all the nurses and doctors, a young woman in the throes of a difficult labor was wheeled by on a gurney. Elvis stopped the gurney, laid his hands on her belly, and tried to absorb the pain into himself. He told her not to worry, that he could feel the child would be born fine.

The next morning, the baby having been delivered without complication as the King had promised, the young woman woke up in the bed next to Sam Thompson's wife. "I had the most beautiful dream last night," she said. "I dreamed Elvis put his hands on my belly and took away my pain." Thompson's wife couldn't bring herself to tell the woman that it hadn't been a dream at all.

One of Dr. Moody's case studies relates a remarkably similar event that occurred two years after Elvis died. A recently divorced Elvis fan discovered she was pregnant and fell into a terrible depression. She did not love the father of her child or want to raise the child on her own, but she couldn't bring herself to have an abortion. When she was wheeled into the delivery room, she recalled, "I had a weird experience. The doctors and nurses were all around me in these white gowns, looking at me. Right there among them, Elvis Presley appeared. He smiled and winked at me. He said, 'Relax, Bess, it's O. K. I'll be here with you.'" When the child was born, it was Elvis who informed her it was a boy. Later, she told Dr. Moody, ". . . I tried to tell my doctor that Elvis had been there with me. The doctor didn't say anything but the nurses chuckled and said I was dreaming. But I wasn't dreaming. It wasn't like a dream. . . . Whatever, I feel like he came through for me when I was feeling so low."

Every year great numbers of the sick, the lame, and the halt make their Lourdes-like pilgrimage to Graceland in wheelchairs and on crutches. Although there's no casting away of crutches at Graceland and it's impossible to know how many of them actually expect to be cured, Graceland provides emotional reinforcement for these souls. This was going on even when Elvis was alive. Larry Geller recalls that during the seventies he "witnessed hundreds of concertgoers carrying their sick or crippled children to the stage and crying out, 'Elvis, please touch my baby,' or 'Elvis, just hold her for a minute.' Few knew of his [spiritual] studies then, and yet thousands apparently sensed that he had some ability to heal."

Bodyguard Dave Hebler wrote, "the worst thing is when someone wheels some poor unfortunate up to the stage in a wheelchair. They tell you that they are dying of leukemia and only have three weeks to live. . . . One incident that sticks out in my mind was this woman yelling for a scarf [from Elvis]. I'm trying to calm her down and ease her out of the way of getting crushed to death and she yells at me, 'But my daughter has got emphysema, don't you understand? She has emphysema.' "

Flora Haas wrote a prose poem entitled "Elvis: Our Flaming Star" (printed in the newsletter of the Chicago fan club, *Elvis: That's The Way It Is*) in which she distills elements of both Elvis' messianic role and miraculous healing powers:

There are too many testimonies of help from Elvis
to be dismissed as just tales.
People who are respectable citizens,
intelligent, educated and not given to fantasy
Have told of his appearing in dreams
and even in visions, to help
With a problem, an illness, a desperate need
or just a lonely heart.

Just as he helped the ill and suffering
during his brief life of 42 years
So is he helping people now,
giving hope and faith in God.

. . . .

Our Elvis is a flaming star of hope, beauty and love
That still sparkles in the nighttime of our suffering world.
Cures of illness have been reported so we believe it's true
That Elvis's spirit lights up our world
and God is letting him renew
Those who turn to him and become one
with the worldwide Elvis family.

. . . .

Elvis is my flaming star and keeps me from thinking of doom.
He also appeared to me in a dream one night now so long ago
And healed my depression that was bringing me
such pain and suffering and my family also.

She ends her poem with a prayer:

Oh, dearest Elvis, you are our flaming star of life, hope and love.
You bring us closer to God just as do the twinkling stars up above.

■   ■   ■

In the same way that Elvis sightings captured the attention of popular media in the late 1980s, angel sightings became ubiquitous media fodder in the early 1990s. The phenomenon even made the cover of the December 27, 1993, issue of *Time*. Declaring it "a grass-roots revolution of the spirit," *Time* reported:

In the past few years [angels] have lodged in the popular imagination, celestial celebrities trailing clouds of glory as they come. There are angels-only boutiques, angel newsletters, angel seminars, angels on *Sonya Live*. A *Time* poll indicates that most Americans [69%] believe in angels. Harvard Divinity School has a course on angels; Boston College has two. Bookstores have had to establish angel sections. In the most celebrated play on Broadway, Tony Kushner's Pulitzer prize–winning *Angels in America*, a divine messenger ministers to a man with AIDS. In *Publishers Weekly's* religious best-seller list, five of the 10 paperback books are about angels.

Time did not draw any parallels between angels and Elvis, but the similarities are notable. Two popular books on angels, Hope Price's *Angels* (originally published in Great Britain) and Don Fearheiley's *Angels Among Us,* both published in 1993, tell stories of angel sightings that are almost identical to the sightings Eicher relates in *The Elvis Sightings.* In many of Price's and Fearheiley's tales of car accidents miraculously averted, sudden cures effected by bedside apparitions, troubled lives turned toward the right path by mysterious but kindly strangers, and so on, the "angels" could be replaced with "Elvis" and the tales would be much like those told by Eicher.

Like witnesses of Elvis apparitions, Price notes that those who experience angel visitations "give every appearance of being honest, ordinary and 'not given to fantasy.' " Elvis lore also comes to mind when seeing that *Time* noted, "Maybe it is not surprising that people who believe they have had an encounter with angels are among the most reluctant to discuss them."

Elvis fan Flora Haas, UFO believers, and those who believe in angels consider the sheer volume and ubiquity of angel sightings to be prima facie evidence of their veracity. "When a remarkably similar event happens to totally unrelated people in different parts of the country," Price writes, "it can only, I think, be genuine." Even *Time* noted "an uncanny similarity in the stories."

Like the Elvis cult, the angel fad is just one of many grassroots religious movements operating outside modern mainstream churches. *Time* cited a priest and a rabbi who considered the angel phenomenon a welcome "backlash against secular society" (each of whom, by the way, had written his own book on angels), but it went on to report that "other clerics are not so sanguine; in many ecclesiastical quarters, the angel revival is a cause for some alarm. Ministers see in the literature the makings of a New Age cult, an easy, undemanding religious faith that may also represent a rejection of mainstream church life."

■ ■ ■

The Catholic Church has been dealing with a grass-roots cult that may be more troublesome than either Elvis or angels: the cult of the Virgin, and the tremendous upsurge in Virgin Mary apparitions over the last decade.

On Sunday, May 3 in 1992, I went to Flushing Meadows–Corona Park in the New York borough of Queens, where the Virgin Mary had reportedly been showing up, to try to catch sight of her myself. In a southern corner of the park, near a bridge vaulting the traffic-filled Long Island Expressway, is a little copse of pine and fir trees shading a circular stone monument that marks the site of the Vatican Pavilion at the 1964 World's Fair. A ceremony was going on there and the monument was decked with red and white roses. A small statue of the Virgin Mary crowned the monument. She too was decked with roses. Men stood behind her holding the stanchions of old-fashioned banners with saints' images on them. Little girls stood around in fluffy white Holy Communion dresses.

A crowd of about two hundred fanned out across the lawn facing the monument. Some knelt on the lawn in prayer, some stood behind baby carriages, but most were elderly, gray-haired folks seated in folding lawn chairs. At the back of the crowd some younger adults bustled about with a video camera on the back of a pick-up truck. Even farther back, in the parking lot, were three or four tour buses whose drivers paced and smoked, killing time.

Everyone in the crowd was dressed in a Sunday church outfit, the men in dark suits, the women in light spring skirts.

More strikingly, all of them, men, women, and children alike, were wearing white gloves and berets. The men's berets were white, the women's blue. It added an oddly rakish fashion touch to the otherwise serious gathering.

A murmuring from the crowd rolled out across the lawn, mingling with the rumble of traffic on the expressway. *Hail Mary full of grace the Lord is with thee. Blessed art thou among women and blessed is the fruit of thy womb, Jesus. Holy Mary, Mother of God. . . .* Most of the people had rosaries draped over their white-gloved hands, and they were telling the beads, one Hail Mary at a time.

This is a scene familiar to me from my Catholic childhood. In Catholic tradition May is Mary's month, and the first Sunday in May we always gathered on the lawn outside our church for a ceremony like this, with rosaries being said and girls in white dresses crowning the Madonna with flowers.

But this ceremony was nowhere near a church. And there was no priest leading the proceedings. These were what Catholics call the laity, and, like much Catholic laity around the world, they were in revolt.

They were the followers of Our Lady of the Roses, aka Our Lady of Bayside, Queens. They claim there are over forty thousand of them worldwide. In 1970 Veronica Lueken, a Queens housewife, had a vision of the Virgin Mary. She's had several hundred of these visions since. Jesus has appeared to her as well. This has made her the center of a Virgin Mary cult well known to New Yorkers, and it's made Queens the nexus of global pilgrimages—"the American Lourdes," it's been called, just as Graceland has. Yet the official Catholic Church refuses to sanction Lueken's story and forbids Catholics from participating in her cult. That's why they meet in this park rather than in a church.

Our Lady of the Roses is an organization that prints some of the messages Leuken receives in one-page flyers called *Directives from Heaven*; they are occasionally handed out on the streets of Manhattan. They typically contain many pleas for Catholics to get back to the old-time religion, but Mary also turns out to be curiously concerned with conspiracy theories. In various communiqués she has warned about global conspiracies perpetrated by the Illuminati, the Freemasons, Pentecostal Protestants, Satanists, Wicca, and purveyors of heavy-metal music. Satan—"not the lesser demons of hell but satan himself"—has walked the earth since 1940, Mary has warned, and he entered the U. S. in 1971. It's not clear where he spent the intervening thirty years.

Through Lueken, Mary has asked good Catholics "to remove all diabolical musical recordings from your homes. Your children are bringing demons into your homes because, at the time that these records were produced, called 'rock,' 'hard rock,' they were produced in the temple of satan—consecrated to satan! You do not understand, My children, but many of your companies, your record companies, are under the control of Wicca, the international organization of witches and warlocks. Do not laugh! It is true!"

The Catholic Church doesn't think so. It has called these messages "products of a fertile imagination."

Not unlike Elvis' followers, Our Lady of the Roses is famous for establishing and maintaining a global grass-roots communication network. Advertisements for its toll-free telephone line, 1-800-345-MARY, were pervasive in New York in the 1980s, appearing everywhere from highway billboards to subway ads. Much like Elvis' fan clubs, the organization developed into a well-oiled pilgrimage machine with a network of pilgrimage organizers that is truly global. The organization has its own travel agency, Rose Tours, and a number of motels and hotels in Queens offer special pilgrimage rates.

Their services in Flushing Meadows share some things in common with the activities at Graceland during Elvis Week as well, such as nighttime candlelight vigils and hymn-singing processions. As of 1992, Lueken stopped making personal appearances; at age seventy, she was in failing health. The faithful carry on without her, just as Elvis' faithful do.

In addition to her Queens appearances, in the early 1990s the Virgin drew as many as ten thousand people at a time to a backyard in New Jersey, about as many to a backyard in Kentucky, and over five thousand to a shrine in Denver (where an appearance by the pope in 1993 drew 375,000). For several weeks in 1990, a thousand a day were drawn to an auto-parts store in Progreso, Mexico, where her likeness appeared on the concrete floor. In the 1980s she appeared to a group of Catholic children in Africa, and in Japan to what Connell called "a group of lay women joined together to live a life of adoration before the Blessed Sacrament." At that site, a statue of Mary wept blood and a deaf nun heard an inner voice prophesying a world destroyed by fire from the sky, i. e., nuclear apocalypse, unless the faithful averted it with their prayers and sacrifices. The nun also experienced stigmata.

■ ■ ■

The Virgin did not appear the day I went to Queens. At least she didn't appear to me. But I can't say with certainty that she didn't appear to any of the true believers at the front of the crowd. Elvis didn't appear in the clouds over Graceland when I was there for Tribute Week. But a lack of a sighting doesn't stop the followers of either cult from continuing to believe and make their pilgrimages and prayers. Festinger's Theory of Cognitive Dissonance posits that a group's strength of faith increases rather than diminishes when its beliefs or expectations are contradicted. In other words, the more one's expectations are thwarted, the greater the faith is needed to uphold the belief.

Angels, Spirit Elvis, sightings of the old-fashioned Virgin Mary—all these visions serve similar needs and longings, such as the need to believe in loving, nurturing powers greater than our own and the longing for a sense of spiritual purpose in a life that can otherwise seem meaningless and sterile.

As mass movements Elvism, angel lore, and the Virgin cult are consistent with other current movements away from traditional establishment churches—with New Age experimentation, for example, and the global rise of old-fashioned fundamentalism in all its forms, from evangelical American Protestantism to Hasidic Judaism to Shiite Islam. It's very easy for outsiders to scoff at the true believers in any of these movements, but perhaps it's ultimately more rewarding to try to understand the motivation behind the convictions of so large and so diverse a group.

The mourning over Elvis' death is approaching twenty years. Beloved deceased spouses and children aren't grieved over for so long or with such dedication. The Florida fan quoted at the beginning of this chapter didn't say it's her late husband she misses "so much," but Elvis. "I never imagined life without him," an Australian fan writes. "I thought he would always be around. When he was taken from this earth, Elvis left a void which, for me, is impossible to fill."

As the years pass it will naturally be increasingly difficult for even the most radical believers to continue to cling to the hope that Elvis is alive. But as Terrina Rush's and Flora Haas' poems indicate, Elvism is well prepared to deal with this. There's always been an aura of the supernatural and the mystical to his sightings that obviates any need for the faithful to believe it's a "live" Elvis who's making appearances. They're miraculous apparitions. The climate for this type of apparition should in fact improve in the coming years when it becomes undeniably clear to all that he's really, really dead.

If Elvis doesn't return in 2001 as Elvis Messiah "To gather us together/For the New World to Begin," his followers may well join the long list of millenarian cults whose faith was strengthened, rather than dashed, when their apocalypse failed to go off as scheduled.

THE
KING'S
MINISTERS

In the beginning was the word and the word was Elvis.
Clayton Benke-Smith, Elvis impersonator

O
N A BITTER COLD winter night in Queens a frigid wind hurtles down the chute of Queens Boulevard with all the jarring momentum of the subway trains rattling overhead on the elevated tracks. Inside the Sunnyside Brauhaus there's the clatter of industrial-weight restaurant dinnerware and the steamy smells of German cooking.

The Brauhaus is a dowdy, drop-ceilinged, hangarlike working-class eatery. In the back of the main room the tables have been pushed aside to clear a small stage area on the floor. Gregg Peters, a smallish guy with hair that looks dyed black and sideburns that look pasted on, sets up his equipment on the old tartan-patterned industrial carpeting. Peters' equipment consists of a small digital tape machine, a guitar, and a couple of small amps—his band in a carrying case.

A little before show time he disappears into the back. A few minutes later, to a digital rendition of Elvis' signature intro vamp, he sweeps out from the kitchen area and struts into the weak spotlights, wearing a Vegas-era jumpsuit and brandishing the guitar. Over the next hour, as waitresses patrol the tables, clearing away dessert plates and delivering pitchers of flat, warm beer, Peters—aka "Little P"—runs through the impersonator's standard Elvis revue, all the hits, from the fifties through "American Trilogy."

It's rough at first not to scoff. He sounds reasonably like the King, has the moves down well enough, and looks vaguely like him if you squint, but ultimately he's just this little guy singing to tapes in the back of a Queens restaurant.

Then, midway through the show, it happens. I'm sharing a table with four friends, and we all see it happen. Something enters the room. Something enters *him*. It is the King's spirit, filling him up like an empty vessel, transforming him into something taller, sexier. For a few amazing moments the Sunnyside Brauhaus is the Las Vegas International Hotel circa 1970, and Little P is fully his Kingship, completely in command of the room, drawing wild cheers from what had been a polite but bored, sauerkraut-sated audience, drawing ladies toward the front to be blessed with the gift of sweaty scarves, drawing us all to our feet for the mighty "Trilogy" finale.

A tiny little boy who can't be more than four years old stands to the side of the stage area, just inside the spotlights. He's dressed in a miniature version of the Aloha-era jumpsuit, complete with a little cape and a big belt. He's studying Peters' moves intently, mimicking the Shaka hand gestures. At one point Little P goes down on one knee, reaches out a hand spangled with costume rings that glitter in the spotlights. The little boy reaches out his own tiny hand and their fingers touch like God and Adam on the Sistine Chapel ceiling. You can almost see the spark of *something* being passed on.

And then it's over. As suddenly as he had descended upon it, Elvis has definitely left the building. The spirit leaves the room in a palpable whoosh, like a pressure drop in the cabin of a jet. The King's spirit has rushed off to some other restaurant or seniors' center or town hall somewhere in the world, where he has an appointment with another faithful impersonator, another empty vessel who needs to be filled up.

The lights come up and the crowd drains out. The Brauhaus is just a dowdy restaurant again. Peters sits at a table and signs small flyers with his photo on them. Asked to sign one as "The King," he quietly refuses. "I'm not the King," he mumbles, "I'm just Gregg Peters," and that's how he signs the flyer.

He's just a little guy with pasted-on sideburns bearing no special resemblance to the King. But upon such rocks as Little P will he build his church.

I went back to see him again a few months later, and this time Elvis' spirit refused to enter him. Little P did the same songs, made the same moves, but never for a moment was he anything other than Little P. His mood was off, his routine rote. He was as empty a vessel when he finished as when he started.

It's like that for Elvii. Sometimes the King enters them, sometimes he doesn't. I've seen several dozen Elvii, some great and some awful, some deadly serious and some just clowning around, little kids and middle-aged men, Elvii of many races and nations.

I've seen some *very* poor representations of the King. Some Elvii just poorly go through the motions. Some Elvii think that it's enough just to curl their lips, shake their legs, and mime the karate moves to recreate the King. At best they come off as vain amateur-hour buffoons or inept Elvis parodists. At their worst, if they're reasonably hunky, or believe they are, or if the women in the audience think they are, they can come off as male strippers at Chippendale's, reducing Elvis' sex appeal and body language to a simple, vulgar hump-and-grind show.

Many Elvii—perhaps all Elvii, when the spirit does not move them—fail to transform rote performance into ecstatic ritual. But there are incompetent priests and shamans in all religions: Catholic priests who just go through the motions of the mass, cantors and gospel singers who sing with technique but no passion.

But I've also witnessed Elvis reaching out and touching one of his anointed, like Little P in Queens or Steve in Memphis, translating him from an ordinary shlump into the King's messenger on earth. I've felt the King's presence electrify a room, transforming it into something like Eliade's sacred space, an ecstatic zone outside of normal space and time.

■ ■ ■

If the Elvis faith develops into a full-fledged religion, the Elvii are there to become its priesthood. They've got the vestments, the liturgy, the ritual, and the faithful congregations. There are Elvii just about everywhere in the world. In addition to North America and Europe, there are Elvii in Cambodia, Indonesia, South America, Mexico, Japan, Taiwan, and Russia. There are Sikh Elvii, Turkish Elvii, Israeli Elvii, and Vietnamese Elvii, and from the Philippines comes "Renelvis, the World's Greatest Philippine-Born Elvis." Thailand is home to several Elvii, including Pol Parsley and Visoot Tungkarat, aka "Elvisoot, the Elvis Presley of Thailand." Every January 8 Elvisoot has the monks at his local Buddhist temple in Bangkok perform a ceremony for Elvis that's usually reserved for venerating the spirits of one's ancestors.

Yasumasa Mori, the Japanese Elvi who caused a stir around the world when he won the impersonators' contest during Tribute Week '93, says his success stems from his getting in touch with Elvis' *ki*—his spiritual essence. Except for England, no culture outside the United States has embraced Elvism as welcomingly and fervidly as Japan.

There are Elvii who grew up with Elvis and Elvii who weren't born yet when he died, male and female Elvii, gay and straight Elvii. A few hundred Elvii, mostly American, show up for the annual competitions in Memphis and Las Vegas. World-wide there are a few thousand serious Elvii, not counting the clown Elvii, the skydiving, scuba-diving, rollerskating, stilt-walking Elvii, or the stripper who calls herself an "Elvis Impussinator."

It could be argued that there are so many Elvii because Elvis is so easy to imitate. Paste on some sideburns, put on a wig, rent a jumpsuit from a costume shop, bring your voice down, learn a few of the moves—how to throw your hip, how to give the Shaka hand sign—you're an Elvi. Few popular figures have become such an easy target.

Some Elvii are in it for the money, others for fun. Some are professional entertainers who've found a niche. But many of them are true believers who got the call to go out and spread the message of Elvis, often at no small sacrifice to themselves and their families. Like peripatetic self-proclaimed preachers of a backwoods Protestant tradition, they hit the road and spread the word because they *have* to.

When Julian "Elvis" Campo was a sickly child in Sicily, he promised God he would do benefit work if he recovered. In 1986 Elvis appeared to him twice and encouraged him in his performing career. Later he made a pilgrimage to Elvis' grave at Graceland, where the King appeared to him a third time to encourage him and also to remind him of the importance of humility. As an Elvi, Campo specializes in charity concerts; his son Angelo "Elvis" Campo performs with him.

Impersonator Artie Mentz recalls, "I had a couple dreams since Elvis passed away, and the one time was where he came to me and he told me that I have to carry on doing what I'm doing. To keep it up. Not to give up. He says rewards will be mine. . . .

"I feel that I didn't choose to do the Elvis show. I feel like I was chosen."

"The day Elvis died I made a promise to myself to keep Elvis' music alive and never let him die," pharmacist and Elvi Bert Hathaway declares. "My goal is to keep him alive forever. . . . Elvis, by far, is the greatest person who ever walked the face of the earth. No one, and I mean no one, will ever replace him."

Bill Cochran says that rather than as impersonator, he'd like to be known as someone who "kept the memory of Elvis alive for people of all ages." Rob "Elvis" Dye says he's a "messenger from Elvis."

Mentz most clearly articulated the Elvi's calling as a minister of Elvis as early as 1984, when he told interviewers in the film *Mondo Elvis:* "An impersonator like myself to Elvis is like a priest to the church. They're giving that live performance, because God is not there in body. We cannot see him. And Elvis is not there in body. We cannot see him. So therefore a priest is like an Elvis impersonator, or vice versa."

Artie and his wife named their son Aaron Elvis, dress him up in Elvis costumes, take him to the Elvis shrines, get him up on stage. "It makes me think of years to come, after maybe I'm not here no more, he'll be goin' on . . . carryin' on the tradition," Artie says.

■　■　■

As the King's ministers, the Elvii have already worked out a thorough and consistent tradition. They have, most noticeably, the Elvis look and vestments. Some Elvii specialize in recreating the young Elvis of the fifties, but they're by far the minority. These Elvii are often young men themselves whose impersonations may well mature into a later period of Elvis' life as they themselves mature. They could be thought of as Elvism's altar boys or seminarians.

The majority of Elvii perform Elvis in his full Kingship, the Elvis of Vegas '69 and *Aloha from Hawaii* and the endless seventies tours. Their Elvis is the Elvis of the jumpsuits and capes and scarves, of the swelling orchestra, the highly stylized ritual of a program of songs and large, hieratic gestures, the ritual the faithful came to know as well as E did.

This was Elvis at his most high priestly. In his book *Elvis People* Ted Harrison noted, "One image of Elvis himself in performance was of the great high priest. His highly decorated costumes bore many similarities to the vestments of the priest presiding at the Catholic mass. Had he been standing behind an altar, his high collars and the spectacular designs on his white jumpsuits could have been mistaken for the garb of a priest celebrating the eucharist."

Elvis' jumpsuits were indeed as glorious and symbolic as an archbishop's ceremonial vestments for high holy days. Any Elvi can tell you their names:

American Eagle	Mad Tiger
Peacock	Black Eagle
Sundial	Red Eagle
Mexican Sundial	Blue Prehistoric Bird
Red Lion	White Prehistoric Bird
King of Spades	Indian
Tiffany	Burning Love
Blue Aztec	Blue Rainbow
Gypsy	Flower
Blue Braid	Flame

Elvii and devout followers know a great deal of trivia about these outfits. Where and when E wore each one; which were his favorites; why he stopped wearing the fringed sash belt as seen in *Elvis: That's The Way It Is;* in which performance he removed his cape and sailed it into the crowd (*Aloha from*

Hawaii); which jumpsuit he was wearing the time he ripped the pant-seat seam, and so on. Different significances are attached to individual outfits. The blue jumpsuits are important because blue is Elvis' color, symbolic of the heavenly blue light Vernon saw when Elvis was born in Tupelo. Mad Tiger relates to Elvis' nickname Tiger Man; both Flame and Indian relate to *Flaming Star*. E looked on the peacock as a mystical symbol of spiritual resplendence and he had stained-glass peacock panels installed at Graceland. The American Eagle is symbolic of E's lifelong patriotism. The Eagle was also the karate nickname he gave to Sonny West (Sonny's brother, Red, was The Dragon), but given the Wests' roles as the Judases among E's apostles, this interpretation of significance is troublesome.

Although it's not entirely formulated yet, these trivia provide the foundation for an Elvist liturgical calendar detailing the symbology of each of these vestments and specifying times of the year when they should be worn at services.

The vestments were certainly not the only aspect of the ceremonial ritual the King left for his Elvii to emulate. He also left them a rote program of songs he repeated with few variations during the many touring years of the seventies. Every Elvi knows the program by heart, and so do the true fans. The ceremony begins with the majestic theme from *2001,* then the band goes into the intro vamp, a simple pair of ascending and descending chromatic triads played over and over as the King/Elvi bounds onto the stage, crosses it, waves and grins to various sectors of the audience, finally settles in the center spotlight and, with a slashing gesture, commands an instant's silence. Then the program of songs begins, each song following another with the regularity and familiarity of any church, mosque, or synagogue service. Even much of the spoken banter between songs is rote, and every good Elvi works some of it into his routine.

The gesturing also follows a ceremonial pattern. The performance of "Poke Salad Annie" requires the Windmilling Arms gesture. "Suspicious Minds" is accompanied by the Strobe-Lit Flash of Both Profiles. There's a specific point in the ceremony when the Karate Fist is called for, another when the Shaka Hand Sign is to be made. If the cape is worn, there's a certain moment in the ceremony when the King/Elvi stands and fans it out in a crucifixion pose.

Although some lesser Elvii overuse it, the all-important Distribution of the Scarves is most properly reserved for the extended ceremonial version of "Can't Help Falling in Love." This is often accompanied by the equally important King's Kiss, when the King or Elvi strolls to the edge of the stage or out among the crowd and allows a few of the women to embrace and kiss him. A variation, sometimes combined with the King's Kiss, is the Kissing of the King's Rings, when Elvis/the Elvi merely extends his jeweled hand to the crowd. Some Elvii bring a few female fans with them to assist in these last parts of the service, but they're often not needed. The fans know when it's time to approach the stage to receive a scarf as automatically as Catholics know when it's time to approach the altar to receive communion.

■　■　■

Elvis left such a precise schematic for the Elvii and the faithful, it's cause for wonder whether he did it on purpose. Why did he put himself through the grueling tours of the 1970s— nearly 1,100 shows in 130 cities in seven years? He certainly didn't *need* to knock himself out trudging from one Podunk town to the next and the next. He could have made much more money much more easily. In his last few years he was visibly killing himself with his tour schedule; he was ill, drugged, bored out of his mind, and deeply depressed. Many were the shows where the Elvis spirit didn't even descend on Elvis.

Toward the end, he could barely stumble his way through a drastically reduced performance.

One theory holds that he spent all this time on the road at the end because he so badly needed the personal contact with his fans; that anything was better than the loneliness of being shut up in Graceland after Priscilla left him, with only specifically scheduled visits from his little Yissa. Another theory is that Elvis spent money as fast as he made it, and after his record sales slumped, touring was the one fast, secure way of making more. And then there are those who contend it was a failure of will: putting E on the road was what the Colonel knew how to do best, and Elvis was too weak willed or too dumb to defy the Colonel.

Maybe it will come to be seen by the faithful as the King's ultimate sacrifice in order to train his followers to carry on after he was gone and that's why he went to all those towns and cities over and over and over again, teaching future Elvii the look, the gestures, keeping the ritual simple and repeating it until they had it memorized.

Toward the end he was barely singing anymore; in his last few years, his performances could hardly be called musical. The pomp and ritual were the whole point: the mere appearance of the King, resplendent in his majestic finery, merely standing there in the lightning of thousands of flashbulbs.

Ultimately, the blessing and distribution of the scarves became the whole focus of the show. Charlie Hodge, his backup singer and sidekick, would scuttle behind him across the stage with an armload of them, like an altar boy chasing the archbishop around the altar. Barely touching them, making a mere show of passing them across his brow, his neck, the King would toss them into the congregation. The mopping of the brow was a purely ceremonial gesture, a scarf draped around his holy neck for a scant few seconds before it was whipped off and handed out to the hysterical crowd, one after another. "Ask, and you shall receive," E was in the habit of saying as he handed them out, clearly playing on the infusion of biblical overtones.

Meanwhile, the King would be barely muttering the words of the song the band was gamely plodding through, rather like the moment in an evangelical meeting when the band plays the verses of a hymn over and over as the faithful stream up to the preacher to be blessed, healed, cured. The music was incidental at that point—it was his presence, his outfits, his touch, his sweat they came for.

Maybe he knew he was parceling himself out to them, a drop of sweat at a time, handing himself out piecemeal to the multitudes. Maybe he really did know he would be leaving them soon and was preparing them to carry on without him. Showing his Elvii the simple, structured rite. *And now. . . the end is near. . . and I must face . . . the final curtain . . . So hush little baby, don't you cry . . . You know your daddy's gonna die . . .*

I am, and I was. Take this scarf, and do this in remembrance of me. For upon this rock 'n' roll I will build my church . . .

In the end, it doesn't really matter whether Elvis thought that's what he was doing, because either way, the Elvists believe it. The notion that Elvis foresaw his departure from this earth is already a solid facet of their lore; the idea that he was preparing his Elvii for it is no great stretch of imagination.

By the 1990s there were many Elvii—probably the majority—who had never actually seen Elvis live. Neither had most of the people in their audiences. During Tribute Week 1994 I sat in the audience of several performances, and when the question was posed to the audience how many had seen Elvis perform, no more than a quarter would raise their hands. Most contemporary Elvii and fans know the performances only through extremely limited concert footage. Elvii study the 1968 tv comeback, *Aloha from Hawaii, This Is Elvis,* and *Elvis: That's The Way It Is* obsessively and minutely as Talmudic scholars. There's not much else in the way of documentation, so it's no wonder so many of their performances are similar pastiches of these four videotapes.

Some say so few of the King's seventies performances (only around a dozen out of the nearly 1,100) were filmed because the Colonel considered concert films useful only as teaser; if he gave the fans too much, they might get lazy and stop buying out the real shows. But some might see this as part of the King's plan. Maybe he purposely left only a handful of primary documents for his Elvii to study, so as not to confuse them. Maybe, as in his live performances, he was intentionally keeping the film footage limited and easy to learn.

It's impossible to overstate the emotional impact of a well-performed Elvis service. The true fans participate with an amazingly powerful willing suspension of disbelief. Good Elvii can reduce women to deep, silent tears or to unseemly displays of raucous enthusiasm; a whole roomful of strangers may link hands and sway together as one, tears streaming down many faces, old and young, male and female.

In the documentary film *Legends* two women fans are interviewed after seeing professional impersonator Jonathan von Brana in Vegas. Both are quietly crying and clearly in a state of high emotion. One's holding a poster of von Brana in a classic Elvisoid pose—a second-generation Elvis icon.

"The King lives again. He was here tonight," one sobs.

"It's like he was just reincarnated every time I see Jonathan," says the other, dabbing an eye, her voice trembling. "He brings back a lot of special memories."

"It makes you feel like Elvis is right there with you," says the first.

"When I saw Jonathan five years ago I was at a very depressed state, because I still couldn't accept Elvis' death," the second testifies. "And to me, Jonathan portrays every good thing, every good aspect that I held dear to me."

Since Elvis' passing, his Elvii, not surprisingly, have created their own additions to his ceremony, and these amendments have already widely become facets of the Elvii liturgy.

One such addition is The Defense of the King. At some point in their ceremony, nearly all Elvii pause for a brief moment of serious talk with the faithful. ". . . I am *sick* and *tired* of all the de*rog*atory remarks about Elvis," as the New York impersonator at the 1994 competition in Memphis declared. Rob "Elvis" Dye says it's part of his mission to be "someone who sets the record straight when people put Elvis down." Some variant on this defender-of-the-faith stance is a standard feature of most Elvii performances, and it always draws a rousing cheer from those assembled. Onward, Elvist soldiers.

Another common and well-received feature is We're All Friends of Elvis Here, a variation on the Christian kiss of peace. This exhortation to group bonding, this affirmation of being the King's chosen people has become another standard rite. It can make for a distinctly chilly moment for anyone present who is suspected, because of their looks or attitude, of not being part of the group.

Serious Elvii emulate the King offstage as well as on. Elvi Clayton Benke-Smith declares, "Any Elvis performer who is dedicated to recreating Elvis' mystique has to eat, sleep, feel, and act like the King." Dave Carlson—whose impersonation Elvis himself enjoyed—says, "You have to look like Elvis, sound like Elvis, and capture all the little idiosyncrasies. But something's got to be there. I can't grab a person's leg and say, 'Here, move your leg like this.' Most of it has to come from the individual."

A trait all Elvii emulate is the King's humility. It was one of Elvis' most revered qualities, and his ministers work very hard to embody it. Many of them may not look much like him, or sing much like him, or possess one iota of his talent, but an impressive number of them—at least the true Elvii—are humble to a fault.

"You can't be Elvis!" Elvi Sammy Stone Atchison declares. "You represent him as professionally and honorably as you can." Pat "Elvis Little" DiSimine says, "I am not trying to *be* Elvis in any way." Joe "Elvis" Eigo insists, "I'm not Elvis Presley. I'm just trying to do the best possible tribute to a great entertainer." And Kim Garner explains: ". . . I don't try to be him. I portray him and I honor him by keeping his music alive."

Even a professional Elvi like von Brana feels some of this spirit. "I love to perform Elvis," he says, "to portray such a humble man. I want to be just like him. I want to grow up to be humble and sweet and nice. . . ." He pauses and grins, "and rich and famous. That's it."

True Elvii are unfailingly polite. Anyone even slightly acquainted with the show-business food chain will find the flawless manners of Elvii startling. They're even respectful to one another; it would be very hard to get an Elvi to say a bad word about another Elvi.

As a function of this politeness, Elvii display endless patience with the fans. Elvii will pose for dozens after dozens of snapshots, striking any Kinglike stance that's asked of them, hours on end, always smiling, always deferential. I've never seen an Elvi refuse to sign an autograph, even if he's pacing nervously on the apron of a stage seconds before show time, or treat fans with any manner of rudeness. Taking time for his fans was something Elvis was never too big to do, at least not until his reclusive final years. "Be good to all my fans," he instructed his Uncle Vester and the other guards at Graceland. "They're the ones who put me on the hill." Fans used to camp out on the lawn during his early years at Graceland; when asked why he didn't have them shooed away, Elvis replied, "I'd never do that. These people have come from all over the world to see me. I wouldn't be in this house if not for them." It's said that he never even locked Graceland's doors in the early years.

"The fans were the living representation of his success," Peter Guralnick writes of the fifties Elvis. "Other stars, he read in the movie magazines, resented the demands that were made on them, but he couldn't understand that. The fans, he said over and over again, were his life's blood. Sometimes he stood out in the driveway [of his former residence on Audobon Drive] for hours signing autographs—they were polite for the most part, and besides, he told *Seventeen* magazine reporter Edwin Miller...'you say no to one person because you had a hundred autographs to sign, they just know you're saying no to them. I never refuse to do anything like that, no matter how tired I am.' Sometimes Gladys would have to call him two or three times to get him to come in for supper."

Elvii also follow the King's example when it comes to charity work and benefit concerts. If it's for a good cause, such as a hospital or other health concern, an Elvi will always be willing to perform. In booking The Night of a Thousand Elvises, a 1994 concert in Baltimore to benefit a homeless out-reach program, the promoter found herself besieged by Elvii from several states offering to donate their services. When listing their major performances, Elvii will list the standard roster of night clubs, trade conventions, county fairs, and so on, but when asked to name their favorite or "most important" gigs, they'll typically mention a charity event where they were proud to be of service and have the opportunity to continue in the King's footsteps.

Just as there are Elvis fan clubs around the world, many Elvii have little fan clubs, too. In *Legends,* von Brana's fans are thrilled when he treats the club to a royal personal appearance. Like the audience at Gregg Peters' show, the club members are mostly middle-aged women, but their husbands are there too, and some seniors (perhaps their parents), and their kids, and some young women as well.

"He only comes down twice a year," a pretty young woman fan complains fondly.

"It's our time with him," the club's president says. A middle-aged woman, she recalls the first time she saw von Brana perform. "At that particular time, my husband got out of the Navy and we divorced. So in order to fill that void, I just kind of switched the focus onto Jonathan and the fan club and the fans."

Asked what she gets out of being the club president, she explains, "A thank you. A smile. 'I'm so glad you came,' or 'I'm glad to see you.' That's all. That's enough."

Club members have bought him Christmas presents, and as he opens them onstage the ladies beam fondly like doting parish ladies fawning on their handsome young minister. Another pretty, young female fan takes the microphone and sings "Angel Baby" to him: "It's just like heaven bein' here with you; you're like an angel, too good to be true . . ."

■　■　■

If Elvii are becoming priests, it should come as no surprise that some Catholic priests act like Elvii. With their long history of cultism and veneration of saints Catholics seem particularly sympathetic or susceptible to Elvism. Fr. John McArthur is a Catholic priest, lifelong Memphibian, and devoted Elvis fan with a parish very near Graceland. He seems set on co-opting Elvis as a saint. He holds an annual gospel mass for Elvis during Tribute Week and fills his church with fans. They call him "Father Elvis."

The gospel choir at McArthur's church does nothing to refute American Catholics' reputation for some of the worst liturgical music ever heard. They sing some of E's favorite gospel tunes—"Precious Lord," "The Old Rugged Cross," "Amazing Grace." Fr. Elvis officiates in blazing white vestments not all that different from an Elvi's jumpsuit. He assures us it is "very appropriate to go to a church" to honor the memory of "Brother Elvis" and "commit him again to a Lord he so deeply believed in." Even "at the moment of his death," he reminds us, Elvis "was reading about the Lord" (the Shroud of Turin book).

Fr. Elvis is already incorporating some important aspects of Elvii liturgy. He looks out at his congregation from the pulpit and says that though some faces are unfamiliar, "there are no strangers here, only Elvis fans." (It's *friends*, father, but that's close enough.) At one point in his sermon he pauses to display a little righteous anger, declaring, "I for one am *tired* of people trying to tear down our heroes." (*Sick* and tired, father.)

Eulogizing Brother Elvis, Fr. Elvis sketches the familiar portrait: a good man, a humble man, a kind man, a devoted son. Fr. Elvis exhorts us to imitate the King's generosity; even though we can't give away Cadillacs and jewels like the King did, "we can give our hearts and our minds. . . . Through your service, through your love, through your daring to be different, you keep Elvis' spirit alive," he instructs.

And the sun will never set on the Son of man.

When it's time for holy communion, the Catholic Elvists proceed down the aisle in their pink fan-club t-shirts, their Elvis earrings—in other venues that week they passed down different aisles to receive a holy scarf from one of the Elvii. Flipping through a prayer book, I find the liturgy normally read at masses for this day, from which Fr. Elvis has deviated for this special ceremony, perhaps out of concern that the customary prayers might suggest some blasphemous analogies. One is from Revelation: "A great sign appeared in the sky, a woman clothed with the sun, with the moon beneath her feet, and on her head a crown of twelve stars. Because she was with child, she wailed aloud in pain as she labored to give birth. Then another sign appeared in the sky: it was a huge dragon, flaming red, with seven heads and ten horns; on his heads were seven diadems. . . . She gave birth to a son—a boy who is destined to shepherd all the nations with an iron rod. Her child was snatched up to God and to his throne. . . ." And from Psalm 45: "So shall the king desire your beauty; for he is lord. . . . They are borne in with gladness and joy; they enter the palace of the king."

At the end of the service Fr. Elvis stands in the back of the church as everyone files out. I find myself blurting out to him, "Thanks, father! That was good!" As though it were a performance. Maybe it was. The distinctions blur.

As it turns out, Fr. McArthur is neither the first nor the only Catholic priest to want to co-opt Elvis. Fr. Peter Madori was a consultant to the Archdiocese of New York's Office of Communications during Elvis' heyday. He was also a big Elvis fan. The night Elvis died, he was a special commentator on ABC radio nationwide.

In an article for *Elvis International Forum* called "Rock My Soul: The Theology of Elvis Presley," he calls Elvis "a genuine American legend." He notes that

> those who know him only as 'Elvis the Pelvis' might find it odd to imagine him in a reflective, ministerial role. . . . [Yet] faith was as natural for Elvis as his suggestive hip-swiveling. In an age when many were questioning the existence of God, he simply took it for granted. What his creed lacked in finesse, it more than made up for in clarity and impact. His theology was not sophisticated, but neither was it simplistic. . . .
>
> Elvis bids fair to be the most popular singer of all time. For some reason, for many reasons, he chose to lend his

considerable clout to popularizing songs about Jesus. . . . Just as Presley's rhythm was gut-level honest, so his gospel was more than skin-deep. It ought to be some solace to his fans—and instructive to all—that Elvis Presley "rocked his soul."

■ ■ ■

Along with Catholicism's possible strategizing to absorb Brother Elvis into its roster of saints, other cross-pollinations could be developing as well. What if, for instance, the Elvii *were* "here to be Elvis"—if in the future there were a syncretic mixing with traditions like Vodun or Santeria, where the priests are literally possessed by their gods? In Santeria ceremonies gods, the orishas, are summoned with drums and chanting, offers of rum and cigars and food. There are points in a Santeria ceremony when the orishas very definitely have entered and "left the building"; they also enter and leave their worshippers, possessing and taking control of their bodies. Fantastic changes are said to come over the faithful when the gods enter them: their voice and posture are altered, they may display extraordinary strength or knowledge, and so on. To outsiders, it can look a lot like the demonic possessions of Catholicism. To an observer of Elvism, it might also look a little like what happens to Elvii like Steve or Gregg Peters when the spirit of the King enters them.

Santeria possession "doesn't happen too often in front of profane eyes," santero Raul Canizares tells me. That is to say, outsiders are no more welcome at Santeria ceremonies than scoffers are at Elvist events.

"The term possession has a very negative connotation in American culture, while the term possession in Santeria has a divine connotation," Canizares explains. "In America, you think Linda Blair and split-pea soup coming out of her mouth. But when you say *possessed* in the context of Santeria, you think of communion with God—or one aspect of God, aspects of divine light."

As a lifelong santero as well as a university professor of religion in Florida, Canizares says he has been possessed by the orishas many times.

> This is how it feels. You begin to lose consciousness, but very slowly. And then, like at a psychedelic movie, you begin to see things shifting around. And then all of a sudden you black out. And then you come to, and you feel very relaxed, very lighthearted. And people tell you that you were possessed, but you don't remember anything that happened. The term "mounted" is used, because you're like a horse and they ride you.

> What happens is, your ego fights with them, and that's why you see all this strange, psychedelic stuff. Your ego is trying not to leave, and they're trying to enter, and then—*oof.* They push your ego aside. Your ego is . . . the analogy would be asleep. You're in a very deep sleep, and you're not sure how many hours have elapsed. When you come to, the time is only like a second for you, but the orisha could have been talking through you for three or four hours.

It's unlikely that any Elvi has such an extreme experience, but if more Elvii come out of Cuban, Haitian, or West African cultures, maybe they will. Meanwhile, deep in the hills of West Virginia lives Jesco White, the subject of the documentary film *Dancing Outlaw.* Though he's not an Elvi per se, he does seem to experience something akin to an Elvist spiritual possession. Like his father before him, Jesco is a "hill dancer," a backwoods version of a tap dancer. He also evidently suffers Multiple Personality Disorder, his three personalities being Jessie (good), Jesco ("the devil in his self"), and Elvis. When Elvis possesses him, he combs his hair and dresses more slickly, speaks with greater self-confidence and flair. In his trailer home he has an Elvis room, part shrine and part "recording studio," where he is surrounded by Elvis icons and music. Elvis, he says, "saved my life." When Elvis possesses him, he feels filled with peace and good will, "just like a burden lifted from me."

H A P P I E S

I thought people would laugh at me.
Some did, and some still are laughing, I guess.

Elvis Presley, 1965

NLIKE JESUS," British observer Simon Hoggart noted dryly, Elvis was "immensely rich, although we must remember that in the US, wealth is generally seen as evidence of God's grace. It is as easy for a camel to pass through the Lincoln Tunnel as it is for a rich man to enter the kingdom of heaven."

Americans do indeed have great respect for wealth, but Elvis is revered not just because he had it, but because he was so lavishly generous with it. Elvis spread his wealth around, first to friends, family, and the Memphis Mafia, but also to charities and complete strangers. It's said that he made $4 billion in his career—and gave away half of it. Nothing pleased him more than giving gifts. He called them "happies."

There are hundreds and hundreds of tales in the Elvist canon relating his gift giving and charity work. His generosity is one of the traits that most endears him to his followers, and it's one of the characteristics they're most apt to cite when defending him against his critics or explaining their idolatry of him. Emulating his charitable nature is a key activity around which the cells of his cult—the fan clubs—have organized themselves.

Elvis himself said that his generosity stemmed from the extreme poverty of his youth, the way his family often depended on the kindness of strangers. One story in Elvis childhood lore, probably apocryphal but repeated as gospel by his faithful, is of a bicycle Vernon and Gladys scrimped and saved to buy for him. Young Elvis took it outside to ride and saw a neighbor boy who was even poorer than he and whose family couldn't afford to buy him a bike. Elvis gave his to this boy. When Vernon and Gladys found out, they praised little E for his generosity and then went and got the bike back. Elvis took it outside and saw the poor neighbor boy again, now feeling even more bereft than he had before. Elvis gave him the bike again.

From the very earliest moments of his career Elvis gave benefit concerts. He gave a benefit concert for a Memphis veteran's hospital just one month after "That's All Right (Mama)" was released. Throughout 1955 he did benefits for and made donations to his alma mater Humes High School, a milk fund for needy kids, police associations, the YMCA, charities for the blind and for convalescent children. At a big charity concert in Memphis on July fourth that year, he donated one of his first diamond rings to be given as a door prize. In 1957 he returned to Tupelo to do a benefit concert in the town where he was born. He also became the March of Dimes' biggest celebrity supporter that year and gave blood to the Red Cross in a highly visible publicity campaign.

E kept giving throughout his career. One of his first live concerts after returning home from the army was a Memphis fund-raiser. His 1961 Pearl Harbor concert raised $62,000 for the building of the USS *Arizona* Memorial, a project that had been stalled for years. His concert raised awareness as well as funds, and work on the memorial was completed shortly thereafter.

His *Aloha from Hawaii* concert in 1973 had a goal of raising $25,000 for the Kui Lee Cancer Fund. Admission to the concert was by a donation of any amount, with E exhorting the audience to give as much as they could. The goal was exceeded by $50,000. In 1975 a benefit concert for hurricane victims in Mississippi raised over $100,000. Little known to nonfans, Elvis also donated portions of souvenir sales throughout his enormously successful stretch of Vegas performances during the seventies, giving an estimated $300,000 to local charities. Back at Graceland he was in the habit of donating $50,000 to Memphis charities every Christmas.

At the 1994 Elvis tribute concert in the Memphis Pyramid, actress Marlo Thomas noted that "Memphis is known for two really great guys: Elvis Presley and St. Jude." She was referring to the St. Jude Children's Research Hospital, which her father, Danny Thomas, had raised funds to build and maintain during his lifetime. He's now buried there. Elvis and Danny Thomas met in the 1950s and discovered their mutual interest in charity work. In 1957 Elvis helped Thomas raise the initial capital to construct St. Jude. In the early sixties Elvis paid $55,000 for the *Potomac,* the 165-foot yacht Franklin Roosevelt used as his "floating White House" during World War II. In its state of dilapidation it might well have perished had he not bought it. He tried to donate it to the March of Dimes and a few other charities, none of which wanted the responsibility of maintaining it, and finally gave it to Thomas to auction off for St. Jude in 1964. The yacht raised $60,000. A portion of the 1994 tribute concert proceeds was earmarked for the hospital as well.

In honor of Elvis' giving to health-care facilities in Memphis, the Elvis Presley Memorial Trauma Center of Memphis' Regional Medical Center was dedicated in 1983. This is the only level-one trauma facility in the region, and it's the only such institution that carries Elvis' name. This public hospital has as its mission the administration of quality care regardless of a patient's ability to pay.

■ ■ ■

In his later years E remarked, "The one thing I bought as a star that meant the most to me was a fifty-dollar picture of Jesus I gave to my parents."

When an interviewer in 1956 asked the young Elvis if he'd let his parents drive any of his four brand-new Cadillacs, the Good Son replied, "What's mine is theirs," without a trace of boastfulness.

During his career he gave away more than a hundred cars. One day he bought nine Lincolns for the boys in the Mafia; another time, he bought them eleven Cadillacs; yet another he bought out a dealership's entire stock of Lincoln Mark IVs in a single weekend. In 1975 his favorite Cadillac salesman awarded him a plaque naming him "The World's Best Car Buyer."

Mary Jenkins was Elvis' cook, maid, and after Gladys' death, surrogate mother. Early in her twenty-six-year tenure at Graceland, Elvis gave her a new car and took her out riding in it. They passed a house for sale that she said she thought was nice. He bought it for her. He wanted to buy all the furniture too, but she insisted on doing that herself. After Elvis died, she furnished a small back room as Elvis' and claimed she often felt his spirit coming there for a rest.

J. D. Sumner and the Stamps, the white gospel quartet who sang with Elvis in his later years, tell a similar tale about the tour bus he bought them, known to fans as the "TCB Bus," which they were still using into the 1990s. He used to ride in it with them, using a bedroom set up in the back. They say there have been many times when they've suddenly felt his presence in that room, like a warm and comforting breeze. One of them likes to sit back there and quietly converse with E's spirit.

A story popularly told is of Elvis seeing a woman wistfully eyeing a Seville when he was at the Cadillac showroom buying Caddies for himself and the boys. Elvis asks her if she likes it, she says yes; he says, Pick out the color you want, it's yours. A radio deejay in Vail, Colorado, hearing the story jokingly announces on air that he'd like one too. Elvis hears about it and sends him one.

Another story—or another version of the same legend—is about Elvis buying a few Cadillacs for himself and close friends on Christmas. Seeing a black couple eyeing the showroom models, he asks them which one they like. They say they can't afford a Caddie, they're just looking. But if you could buy one, which one would you buy? he asks them. They point one out. He tells the salesman, Give them the keys and add it to my bill.

Larry Geller recalls, "Among the numerous beautiful presents I received from him were a black sapphire ring . . . a Cadillac, a motorcycle, a mobile home, a five-gaited quarterhorse, a pickup truck, and countless articles of his clothing. . . .

"Of course, there's no question that Elvis could afford to give everything he gave away, but, knowing him as I did, I can safely say that even had he lived out his life as an obscure truck driver he'd still have given things away. Not cars, of course, but whatever he had."

In 1966 Elvis bought a ranch in Mississippi, named it the Circle G (for Graceland), and proceeded to buy horses, jeeps, pickups, and mobile homes for his entire entourage. One day Mafioso Alan Fortas pointed out to Elvis that he'd bought one more pickup than there were hangers-on to give them to. E gestured distractedly to the crowd of fans who were always gathered outside the ranch's front gate and said, "Alan, damn, man, just give one away to one of them. Don't bother me with details like that!"

Elvis bought piles of jewelry for his friends and family, choosing gems for each person according to astrological and numerological significance. J. D. Sumner's left hand was called "Elvis Presley's hand," because on his fingers he wore over $100,000 worth of jewelry given him by the King. In concert Elvis would tell Sumner to hold up his right hand and show it to the audience. Then he'd say, "Now hold up *my* hand," and Sumner would flash the jewelry for the audience, who always went wild.

At one concert Elvis showered the audience with an estimated $35,000 worth of gold and diamond rings. At another, Elvis was handing a man a scarf when the man shouted to him, "I don't want the scarf. I want the ring," pointing to a $10,000 item on one of Elvis' fingers. Elvis slipped it off and handed it to him.

At Christmastime the Memphis department store Goldsmith's would open late at night just for Elvis to go on a gift-shopping spree. He loved showering his entourage with Christmas happies. According to one anecdote, his favorite gift he received was a candy bar his cousin Harold Lloyd sent him every year without fail. It was a reminder of their childhood poverty, and E always thanked him for it sincerely.

One Christmas Eve Elvis took a few of the Mafia on a count-your-blessings tour of the Memphis city jail. To his surprise, he discovered a former Humes classmate behind bars. E immediately paid his bail and had him released so he could be with his loved ones for the holiday.

The stories are endless.

- Elvis reads an article in a Memphis paper about a crippled black woman who can't afford a wheelchair. He buys her the most expensive model available and personally delivers it to her humble house.
- Stopping at a red light in downtown Memphis, Elvis sees a man selling pencils on the corner. He leaps out of the car and stuffs a few hundred-dollar bills into the man's cup.
- A man stops along the road to help Elvis fix his car. Elvis takes his name and address. The next time the guy goes to make his monthly mortgage payment, he discovers that Elvis has paid the mortgage—in full.
- A man who'd been a major figure in country music when Elvis was coming into his own visits Graceland years later. He is now down on his luck. Elvis gives him a check for $5,000. The man leaves in tears.
- After record producer Felton Jarvis spends two years waiting for a kidney transplant, Elvis steps in and arranges one in six days.

- When Jackie Wilson, whom he greatly admires (and from whom he ripped off a move or two), has a heart attack, Elvis puts $30,000 toward his medical bills.
- In his home in Bel Air during the Hollywood years, Elvis sees a telethon on a Los Angeles tv station and has someone make a call with an offer to donate half again the final amount on the tote board. His gift: $85,000.
- Two English girls who've visited him in Bel Air a few times show up one day in tears. Working in Beverly Hills, they'd saved up for three years to bring their father over from England. He arrives and promptly dies of a heart attack. They've spent every penny they had to fly him over. Elvis tells them not to worry; he'll take care of everything. Later, they come back to the house and hand him an envelope. When he opens it, tears start streaming down his face. They've brought him $5 as a first install-ment toward paying him back. "No one's ever tried to pay me back," he tells them. "No honey, you keep the money. You've already paid me back more than you'll ever know."

"A lot of people think he does those things for publicity, but he doesn't," Red West admitted. "When he gives, he really gives. It's a genuine gift and he doesn't announce it."

"No one will ever know the number of people whose businesses he rescued, or the tornado victims to whom he sent house trailers, or the destitute whose hospital bills he paid. He thought that's what money was for," says *Reader's Digest*.

"He felt the Good Lord blessed him when he gave to others," recalls his friend Ed Parker. "For this reason he gave so impulsively. He always felt his talent was given to him as a gift from our Lord. He felt he should share that gift with others, whether through his voice or through monetary means. He gave for the joy and self-satisfaction that stemmed from giving."

At a Humes Middle School (formerly Humes High School) gathering during Tribute Week '94, members of the Mafia told many stories about how "caring and giving" Elvis was. "He liked to share his wealth," Joe Esposito remarked. And then it sounded like he said "He was one *superhuman being* when it came to that. He cared about people more than himself."

Later I realized he'd said "one super human being," but a hundred years from now, Elvist scripture will probably record the former version anyway.

■ ■ ■

Red West, not surprisingly, pointed out what he thought was a dark side to all of Elvis' giving, "one of the most curious and puzzling things about Elvis. I have seen him give away some of the most incredible gifts imaginable. In later years he was to give away clothes and cars and rings, and even airplanes and houses, but he likes to be in control. Gifts are one thing. Money is something else. The point is that I believe somehow he believes money gives a person independence. He doesn't want people to have independence from him. He likes to be a father figure, or a God figure."

Among sedentary agricultural societies in preindustrial cultures there is a primitive mode of organization called the "big-man" system. Best known in Melanesia and New Guinea, "big men" goad their villages to increase production and savings by promising to throw a big feast with the resulting surplus. "When the feast takes place, the 'big man,' surrounded by his proud helpers, ostensibly redistributes—parcels out—piles of food and other gifts but keeps nothing for himself," according to anthropologist Marvin Harris. Under the right circumstances, big men become the nucleus of a new ruling class.

In New Guinea, a young man who wants to become a big man first inveigles his family into working toward a feast. If it's a success, he attracts a wider circle of people, who then work to make an even bigger feast. He in turn must keep raising the level of his generosity to meet the increasing size of his circle of "friends." Often he will build, Harris explains, "a men's clubhouse in which his male followers can lounge about and in which guests can be entertained and fed."

Eventually the big man feels strong enough to challenge other big men in the vicinity to a kind of feast duel—a food fight, as it were. He invites his rival to a big feast; the rival then has a year to work toward throwing an even bigger one. "At the end of a successful feast, the greatest [big man] still faces a lifetime of personal toil and dependency on the moods and inclinations of his followers," Harris writes. He is constantly challenged to do more, to be bigger.

His followers reap the benefits of their toil in feasting, but the big man is required to be selfless and abstinent, giving away all that he has goaded them to produce for him. On one island there's a saying, Harris reports, "The giver of the feast takes the bones and the stale cakes; the meat and the fat go to the others."

One old New Guinean recalled, "If [the big man] didn't furnish us with women, we were angry. . . . All night long we would copulate and still want more. It was the same with eating. The clubhouse used to be filled with food, and we ate and ate and never had enough. Those were wonderful times."

In regaling us with stories of their glory days with the King at his various "clubhouses" in Graceland, Vegas, or Hollywood, Red, Sonny, and the rest of the Mafia are a little like that old New Guinean. The orgiastic, gluttonous side of the King is often cited by nonbelievers as a serious objection to the esteem his followers have for him. Elvis' faithful, on the other hand, have little trouble with the notion that the King and the boys enjoyed the fruits of popularity. If anything, they're envious. Excess goes hand in glove with success in America. As though they were vicarious members of the Memphis Mafia, Elvis fans share, in a distant way, in the big man's largesse.

Anthropologists point out that there's something pre- or even anticapitalist about the big-man system. Capitalists don't cajole their friends into working for them; they hire employees. And they aren't compelled to redistribute the surplus to them; they pay them a fixed wage.

In a sense Elvis, like most pop stars, was a small businessman. And small businesses are often run by the big-man philosophy. Employees are often friends and family. Because of his closeness to them, the employer feels compelled to distribute largesse beyond the impersonal exchange of wages for labor.

Elvis, for all the money he made and spent, was never a capitalist, and most of his entourage worked for nothing like a fixed wage. There was much about the big-man culture he created that has southern, working-class, anticapitalist roots, which no doubt made it appeal especially to fans from nonentrepreneurial social strata.

■ ■ ■

"Elvis was so warm and caring," one fan says. "The public should never forget this. In Elvis' name I give. . . ."

"The charity work the fans are doing is one of the most positive ways to keep the memory of Elvis alive," says another.

Doing good works "in Elvis' name" is an obligation all of his American fan clubs take very seriously. They're not only emulating him but traditional church group activity as well. They also use their altruism to counter the lies and slander about Elvis they see in the media. (Groups elsewhere in the world have generally been less avid about charity work, but years of American fan clubs' evangelizing are changing that. A Belgian fan club is said to be particularly active in charity work.)

American fan clubs are constantly holding raffles, dances, memorabilia sales, bingo parties, and so forth to benefit various charities. While they focus particularly on the Trauma Center and other Memphis charities, they also give to their hometown institutions. The funds they raise aren't as enormous as the amounts established churches are able to generate, but they show signs of a steady increase. In its first ten years, the Trauma Center received an estimated total of $125,000 from Elvis' fan clubs; as of 1994 Memphis' Le Bonheur Children's Hospital had received around $100,000. The Burning Love fan club of Illinois is said to be the leading fund-raiser, contributing as much as $15,000 a year to the Trauma Center and Le Bonheur. The We Remember Elvis club in Pittsburgh is another busy fund-raiser. In 1991 at their annual convention on "Elvis Day" (April 27, which they had persuaded the mayor some years earlier to declare officially) they raised $4,500 for a local burn-trauma unit. They've also created an Elvis Aaron Presley Visiting Fellowship at the burn-trauma unit, funding training for doctors from other countries.

Most fan clubs are smaller and their donations, regularly applauded in *Elvis International Forum,* are considerably more modest: $102 to the Trauma Center from the Presley-ites fan club in Florida; $1,000 from Elvis Memphis Style; $500 to the American Diabetes Association from the True Fans For Elvis club of Maine; $100 to a local high school from Elvis Friends Are The Best, an Amarillo, Texas, club; and so on.

Every year fan clubs around the world send teddy bears to the kids at Porter Leath Children's Home, a Memphis charity Elvis always supported. There's a similar Teddy Bear Caravan in Atlanta every year.

"Some Elvis fans have, on occasion, endured ridicule for their passion," Cindy Hazen and Mike Freeman report in their book *The Best of Elvis.*

Robin Rosaaen, Public Relations Liaison for The Elvis Special Photo Association of California, made an appearance on "The Oprah Winfrey Show" in 1991. On the air, Robin described her collection of Elvis memorabilia which she values at a quarter of a million dollars. Oprah reacted in disbelief and an audience member declared she had wasted her money.

What they didn't know is that Robin uses her collection to raise money for charity. In 1990 she staged a three-day exhibit of her memorabilia at a San Francisco Bay area hotel. Adults were charged five dollars and children two dollars to see her collection. Proceeds went to Meals on Wheels and other charities.

The president of the Burning Love fan club, also a big collector, told Hazen and Freeman, "Every item I own is very precious to me, but not as precious as preserving Elvis' memory. I don't believe in recognition. Elvis never asked for recognition. I do it because it's so rewarding."

Corporate Graceland and Elvis Presley Enterprises have gotten into the act. Working with fan clubs, Graceland auctions Elvis memorabilia and sponsors a karate tournament to benefit Le Bonheur, organizes a Tribute Week 5K Run to benefit United Cerebral Palsy, and hosts a dinner to benefit the Make A Wish Foundation. With Memphis' Then, Now And Forever fan club, Graceland supports Humes Middle School under the Adopt A School program. It also stages benefits and makes contributions to the Trauma Center, St. Jude's, the Johns Hopkins Children's Cancer Center in Baltimore, and other charities.

A *Reader's Digest* article covering Elvis Week '93 related the following story:

A family of four stands across the highway from Graceland, mother, father, teen-age son and daughter. Everyone in the crowd swirling around them has a destination: the bus to the house, the tour of Elvis's airplanes, the auto museum. Only these four stand, gazing with undisguised longing across the highway.

A Graceland employee approaches: "We're doing a

survey. Could you tell me where you live?"

The father smiles ruefully. "We don't live anywhere. We're on the road until I find work. But right now we're just taking in Elvis."

"You mean you don't have tickets to any of the tours?"

"No, ma'am."

"Please don't go away." She runs off and is back in minutes with tickets. "Be our guests," she says, "and God keep you."

As trustees of the estate EPE cannot give away Cadillacs. But they still try to do things Elvis would like.

■   ■   ■

When the Memphis Mafia gathered at Humes Middle School during Tribute Week '94, they took questions from the audience. One working-class man, tall and wiry and gray-haired, stood up and asked, "How did you get to be a member of the Memphis Mafia?"

Up on the stage, the Mafiosi—Joe Esposito, George Klein, Linda Thompson's brother Sam—hemmed and hawed, obviously uncomfortable with the unstated insinuations in the man's question. Well, Esposito finally explained, there wasn't any official entry process or anything; you just had to be, well, one of Elvis' friends.

"But how did you get to be one of Elvis' friends?" the man persisted. The question was heavily freighted—what he really wanted to know was, How is it that you guys, a bunch of good ol' boys just like me, entered the charmed circle? How is it you got to party at the right hand of the King, savor the King's largesse of women, jewels, Caddies? What did you do to deserve the good life nonpareil? Although his question was posed in the past tense, the man's longing was very much present tense. Having missed out on the extraordinary fortune that was the King, he was hoping they might reveal some secret to their luck, something he might use to score for himself. His query was eschatological; beneath the question of *how* he might cash in was the question of *when*.

In America the rags-to-riches story is the most attractive means of wealth, because it implies that anybody might be so blessed. Half of the appeal of Elvis' lavish gift giving is fantasizing what it would be like to be a recipient; the other half is fantasizing about having so much to give.

Marxism maintains that consumer capitalism raises the desire for commodities to an essentially pagan kind of worship, a "commodity fetishism." The simple desire for worldly goods is transformed into something more like religion when *hope* is associated with the goods. By imbuing commodities with magical properties beyond their actual utility the desire to obtain them can be rationalized. The enthusiastic encouragement of advertising implies that the mere acquisition of these totemically charged objects—Cadillacs, Lincolns, diamond rings, whatever—magically improves a person.

It is Cargo Cultism, American style. Cargo Cults have been the subject of at least two movies, *Mondo Cane* and *The Gods Must Be Crazy*. These films describe Cargo Cults as having been formed by innocent primitives who out of awe for the technological magic of superhuman white people naively worship the white man's tools and mimic white behavior. But this interpretation misrepresents the motivation behind these cults. Cargo Cults were formed not as a reaction of awe, but of envy and frustrated desire.

Cargo Cult activity began with the arrival of white European colonials in the South Pacific, Papua New Guinea, and the Melanesian islands in the late 1800s. Recruited as low-wage laborers, natives built docks, roads, airstrips, and entire new towns under the direction of white bosses. They watched as the cargo ships and planes arrived, as if by magic, from some unknown, far-away place, and disgorged a miraculous cornucopia of goods—refrigerators, sewing machines, motorcycles, trucks, rifles, crates of canned goods, prefab buildings that seemed to erect themselves overnight.

"As far as the natives were concerned," anthropologist Peter Worsley writes, "the Whites received the goods by steamer from unknown parts; they did not manufacture them, and merely sent pieces of paper back. They did not apparently work themselves, yet refused to share their fortune, forcing the natives to work long and hard for a return of a small proportion of the goods they themselves obtained with such ease and in such profusion. Who made these goods, how and where, were mysteries—it could hardly be the idle White men."

The natives became obsessed with the idea that the whites were keeping from them the secret processes that produced and delivered all this wonderful cargo. They were convinced that the secrets were contained in pages that white missionaries must have ripped out of the Bibles they distributed. They believed that the missing pages were where their ancestors and heroes explained how the whites were magically interdicting the cargo shipments and keeping it all for themselves.

Cargo Cultists began to copy the way the whites acted, dressed, and spoke, understanding their behavior to be ritual magical practices for the procurement of wealth and prosperity. Some Cargo Cultists created crude "radio towers" of scrap lumber and vines to communicate with their ancestors in the sky, as they'd seen the whites doing. They cleared small "air strips" in the bush or built their own ramshackle docks in undeveloped harbors to receive the cargo when it arrived by air or sea. Simple huts were raised and designated a village's *faktori* and *ofis,* in Pidgin English; cultists organized themselves into *komitis,* with some people known as bosses and others as *wokas.*

In some villages the natives slaughtered all their pigs, stopped tending their crops, and set up banquet tables out in the open, where they sat doing absolutely nothing, just like they'd seen white people do, waiting for a miraculous meal to be brought to them. In other villages, men organized themselves into "armies" and carried sticks, which they believed would be replaced by real weapons when the cargo came. Then they would overthrow the whites who'd been cheating them for so long.

To suppress the cults, colonial governments often arrested the leaders and banished them for life to distant islands. When reports came in that these leaders had died in exile, their followers refused to believe it. A legend spread that one banished leader, who had in fact died in exile, continued to communicate with his chief disciple by sending him letters that fluttered down from the sky and landed on the tip of his "bayonet." That both the receiver of these messages and the alleged writer were illiterate was irrelevant to believers. The cultists believed that the colonials had tried to murder another leader who also died in exile by throwing him down the smokestack of a cargo-bearing steamship, but that he had survived and would be returning one day as a messiah, bringing lots of cargo with him.

When the cargo finally arrived, many cultists believed, it would herald the beginning of the apocalypse. The whole order of the cosmos would be overturned; the earth would quake, the seas would boil, and Satan, whom the cultists identified with the whites, would be bound up. The islanders would become the rulers of the whites, making the whites do the hard work while they themselves sat back and enjoyed the prosperity.

The view of Cargo Cultists as ignorant primitives is not very distant from the view of Elvis cultists as ignorant trailer parkers. But, as folklorist Ted Daniels points out, Elvists are not the only people in this country who have Cargo Cult–like notions. "For example," Daniels says, "there's a lot of talk about 'free energy.' Absolutely cost-free as well as pollution-free. Nicola Tesla is supposed to have invented it and then died, and of course nobody can figure out his notes. Or 'they' destroyed them. And are you old enough to remember when nuclear power was going to be too cheap to meter?" He cites as well the UFO lore that "the aliens have brought us the technology for space flight, but they're keeping it under wraps in Nevada."

The Cargo Cult notion that secret pages were ripped from the Bible is not at all foreign to this country as well. Daniels notes that a lot of people believe that "translators leave stuff out, or they change things, so only the pope knows what's really in the Bible. And of course," he chuckles, "how do we know they didn't?"

Many people of Western culture engage on a daily basis in a kind of magical thinking not unlike the Cargo Cultists: they dress for success and emulate the behavior of rich white people, in the hope of attracting some of the cargo to themselves. People of the middle class aspire to the high life of the rich and famous and are compelled to copy their modes of dress, dine in the same chic restaurants, become autodidactic experts in French wines, Italian fashion, exclusive resorts. Hip young people wear grungy clothes, get tattoos, affect suicidal depression and world-weariness, with the hope that by dressing and acting like artists and poets and rock stars they will become (or be *as good as*) them.

To some extent we're all Cargo Cultist. The Elvists are just more honest about it, as they wait for their Elvis messiah to return to them, bringing lots of happies. They seem far less conflicted about it than many mainstream churches that equate the desire for worldly goods with a temptation to sin—or in fact consider it the very root of all evil. Elvists, by contrast, in no way disapprove of Elvis' having amassed, enjoyed, and spread his wealth around. Rather than a temptation to evil, his wealth empowered him to do good in the world, and it inspired his followers to do good "in his name." Elvism implicitly equates "living the good life" with living a good life in the moral sense. Elvism may be the first true consumer-culture religion, born and spread in a consumerist milieu, and thoroughly consonant with consumerist ideals.

ICONS,

RELICS,

AND SHRINES

Recorded . . . in the 60th year of our Lord, Elvis Presley.
liner notes, Same Old Story, *The Hangdogs*

I N JANUARY 1995 Elvis entered my building. He came to me
in my time of need. I was organizing my notes for this
chapter, thinking about his relics and icons, and he brought
the relics and icons to me. A huge auction of rock 'n' roll
memorabilia, including a large cache of Elvis items, came to
the Puck Building, where I work, in New York City. Thank
you, E.

I knew what the King wanted me to do. The morning the
items went on display prior to the auction, I was one of the
first four people in the room. Glass-fronted display cases filled
with Elvis items had been set up at the far end of the room.
For record collectors and dealers the main attraction was some
four hundred Elvis acetates, coated-aluminum "reference
recordings" made before mass production of a vinyl record.
Only one to five acetates of a recording were made, and they
can be played only a few times before they deteriorate, so
they're rare and highly prized by collectors. They look like
normal vinyl records except for their industrial labels with
handwritten or typed titles.

The highlight of these was touted as "the earliest known Elvis acetate," from the 1954 session when E paid $4 to record "I'll Never Stand in Your Way" and "Casual Love Affair" for Sam Phillips. Supposedly Elvis took the only acetate home with him and later gave it to a relative, who later gave it to someone else to settle a debt. Not mentioned in the auction catalog, which valued it at $250,000, was the rumor that RCA disputed the authenticity of this story.

Others had as much intrigue, if not collector value: an alternative version of "That's All Right (Mama)"/"Blue Moon of Kentucky" made for a Memphis radio station (possibly for Dewey Phillips, the deejay who first broke Elvis locally); acetates of "Baby Let's Play House" and "Love Me Tender," "His Latest Flame" and "You'll Never Walk Alone," "G. I. Blues" and "Viva Las Vegas," "Devil in Disguise" and "Blue Christmas," and so on, spanning his career.

The real relics, however, were in other cases situated around the room. All bearing numbered auction tags disturbingly reminiscent of toe tags in a morgue were such items as a pair of Elvis' sunglasses, with the letters *EP* on the nosepiece and TCB lightning bolts on the earpieces. Several of his massive gold and diamond-studded rings were on display, along with one of his leisure suits, one of his credit cards, a couple of pillows from Memphis, his karate bag, earmuffs he wore on the pistol range, an electric shaver, some handwritten letters and postcards, some framed autographs. A blue motorcycle helmet of his looked awfully small—did *that head* really fit in there?

Trying to feel some emanation, I leaned close to the cases, but the relics were inert and unremarkable as any old junk in a flea market or estate sale. Just old *things*. The only tremors I felt were from the subway trains below.

Maybe it was the philistinic, money-lenders-in-the-temple setting. When the auction was held a few mornings later, I ran into a handful of true Elvis fans. Darwin Lamm of *Elvis Interna-*

tional Forum had come from California. Photographer Ed Bonja was there with some huge, beautiful prints of his famous concert shots; many of the best-known seventies-era photos of Elvis at the height of his Kingship, caped and jumpsuited, are Bonja's work. Two or three other true fans were there, all middle-aged men who'd been fans for decades. We stood in a corner in the back, and they were clearly experiencing the same low vibes I had.

The room was full of local, national, and BBC tv crews. About a hundred people were bidding, but it was all very low-key and businesslike. The participants were record collectors and dealers, not fans or believers. They were there on business. There was absolutely no sense that anyone was excited to be in the room with the relics. One fan told me it was nothing like the spirit at the June 1994 auction where Jimmy Velvet, for years the well-known impresario of a traveling museum of Elvis memorabilia, was selling off a portion of his huge collection. The fans had turned out for that one, this fan told me, and they "were like sharks in a feeding frenzy. The guy could have held up a cigarette butt and they would have snapped at it." Even the *Wall Street Journal* caught some of the spirit at that auction; "Elvis Relics Fetch Big Bids at Vegas Sale," read the headline to the article covering it.

Even the New York City philistines couldn't help getting excited about a few of the star items on the block. One was a two-minute color reel of an eight-mm home movie capturing Elvis onstage at a place called Magnolia Gardens in 1955. It was billed as some of the earliest-known "live" footage of him. The young Houston man who was selling it told me the story behind it. In 1955 his mother and father were celebrating their first wedding anniversary at the Magnolia Gardens, and his mother happened to have her camera with her when she saw some guys pull up in a big car. It was Elvis, Scotty Moore, and Bill Black. She didn't think of them as anybody special, but since she was practically at the front of the stage, she shot a few minutes of their performance. The footage shows a very young Elvis in a blue short-sleeve shirt holding a very large guitar, cranking up one of his early rockabilly numbers. The filmstrip is soundless, but by studying his lips it would probably be possible to tell which song it is. Something about the film's silence makes it all the more fascinating—it's like gazing at an icon that moves.

When the bidding for the film got under way, it was heated. All the tv cameras turned their blinding lights on the action, and applause broke out at the end for the winner, who bid $12,000. The Elvis fans I was standing with shrugged and shook their heads; the winning bid was way under the $40,000 to $60,000 the owner had hoped to get. Perhaps the film's restricted commercial use had some bearing on its price. Attached to the film was a serious disclaimer that it was being sold for private use only and that any copying, distribution, or commercial use of any kind must be licensed from Elvis Presley Enterprises, Inc.

The auction drizzled on. No one bid at all on the highest-ticket items: they passed on the $250,000 acetate, E's $28,000 sunglasses, one of his silk shirts. Bidding was more lively on other items. E's Humes High School library card went for $650; his tenth-grade yearbook for $3,750; a horseshoe ring Vernon gave him went for $5,500; a jacket he wore in *Clambake* for $6,500; a postcard he sent from Germany for $1,500; one of the gold watches he used to give the Mafia, $4,500; a watch he gave to Priscilla on their wedding day, $1,400; the motorcycle helmet, $550; a tour jacket, $450. The fans kept shaking their heads at these unheard-of, rock-bottom prices. At the Velvet auction, a pair of E's sunglasses had gone for over $26,000, and an authentic jumpsuit for $68,500.

Some items drew laughter from the crowd. There was a mammoth bedspread made of regal red velvet with gold tassels, which Elvis kept on his bed in Graceland in the early seventies. "What size is it?" a bidder called out. "King-size, of course!"

someone else quipped. No one wanted a nativity scene that had stood on the Graceland lawn for just one holiday—Elvis had it replaced because he thought the Virgin Mary looked like a tart. Throw pillows from Graceland on which the King most likely had rested his head drew only snickers and bargain-basement bids; true fans would have been much more excited.

Just before I left, one of the Elvis fans told me a story, an ominous reflection on the whole event. During one of his seventies concerts Elvis removed his cape and belt buckle and handed them to a little seven-year-old fan. The kid kept them as he grew up and then traded them to Jimmy Velvet in return for a brand new Trans Am, which he proceeded accidentally to crash into a tree, killing himself.

■ ■ ■

Long before the religiosity of Elvists was widely acknowledged, their penchant for acquiring and enshrining sacred relics and icons was a hallmark of the faith. The merchandising of celebrity memorabilia has been a lively industry in America for some two hundred years, dating back to large sales in George Washington commemorative ceramics and Ben Franklin ceramic dolls. But the Colonel took it to dizzying heights even P. T. Barnum would've admired. There are collectors of icons and totems associated with nearly every kind of pop star today, and even a few modern martyrs like JFK have been the focus of household shrines. But for no modern popular figure is the practice of collecting memorabilia carried out with quite the avidity or reverence as among Elvists—the auction among the New York City philistines notwithstanding.

Forty years after girls first fought over scraps of his clothing and the Colonel realized there was a market for *anything* with E's likeness or name on it, E's iconography continues with amazing persistence to spread around the world. When he's not on the cover of *Life* for his sixtieth birthday, Elvis will be mentioned in a newspaper article, often just as an aside.

Travelers run into museums of relics actually touched by the King in cities and towns around the world. Or for the sedentary there are touring exhibitions like Jimmy Velvet's mobile museum. One of E's gold-appointed Cadillacs toured the world by itself, a golden chariot fit for a sun god.

Tens of millions of Elvis stamps have passed through the mail since 1992, making this icon one of the most ubiquitous in the United States.

On tv every evening the chances are very good that at least one, if not two or three, Elvis references will pop up. On an average shopping day, making the usual rounds to the supermarket, the shoe repair shop, the hardware store, the gas station, it would almost be impossible not to encounter the image of Elvis, perhaps in a small Elvis shrine in the back of a shop, or as a poster on a wall. This is true for New York City, small southern towns, and Anytown suburbs alike. He's there, somewhere, every day.

The fact is that Elvis' image and Elvis references are more common and multifarious today than they ever were when he was alive. Astonishingly, the proliferation *increases* with each passing year since his death. Elvis is more of a presence today than he was five years ago, and his imagery is very likely to be even more pervasive five years from now.

Naturally, not every reference to Elvis is religious, and not every Elvis poster, commemorative plate, or velvet tapestry is an object of worship—though it could be argued that they're all objects of reverence. Elvis is a *cultural* icon for many more people than he is a religious one. He is a global touchstone, a universally recognized ideogram in the multimedia lingua franca of pop culture.

Very early on the universally mocked velvet Elvis paintings came to symbolize to outsiders everything that was tacky and low-class about Elvism. Of course velvet Elvis *is* tacky. So is virtually all popular religious iconography produced on all continents and in all religions, be it Mexican religious art, Italian holy cards, the Tibetan mountains defaced with sacred grafitti, or the figurines, calendars, and toys of popular Chinese Buddhism.

The proliferation of velvet Elvises is nothing compared to the proliferation of Elvis images that are specifically, intentionally religious in nature. Many are commercially produced, others are homemade. Elvis in heaven, sometimes with Vernon and Gladys, sometimes standing at pearly gates that look much like Graceland's gates, is a favorite theme. Another is Elvis as the Aloha Colossus, bestriding the blue planet, beaming his message to all humanity.

Noncommercial Elvist artists are working toward a standardization and universalization of his icons. They tend to emphasize and exaggerate the androgynous qualities of Elvis' features: his eyes and lips are often enlarged, the soft, feminine qualities even more pronounced than in life, his lips look glossy and "kissably soft," his eyelashes are so heavily mascaraed that his eyes look like those of a temple prostitute. Always polymorphous in his sexuality, in the idealized divine state envisioned by his worshippers, Elvis is clearly moving toward the pure omnisexuality of deities such as Krishna, Dionysus, Antinous, and the postmedieval Jesus, among others.

Ralph Wolfe Cowan, the painter Elvis commissioned to create the godlike portrait of him that hangs in Graceland, has made far more blatantly idolatrous images since E's death. A famous painting Cowan made in 1988 is called *Praying Elvis*. It has been reproduced on a Christmas card that is sold in shops across the street from Graceland. It shows Elvis in profile, wearing his priestly white jumpsuit, his hands folded in prayer. His eyes are closed, his face composed in humblest supplication. Behind him is Cowan's trademark cathedral of golden cumulus clouds. A faint but unmistakable halo encircles E's head and shoulders. Inside, the card reads:

A gentle prayer for Christmas,
A gentle prayer of love,
All my fondest wishes
Coming from above.

In the Arab-Israeli village of Abu Ghosh, Israel, there are two religious shrines—neither of them Moslem or Jewish. One is a fifth-century church with a giant statue of the Virgin Mary. The other is just down the road: the Elvis Inn, where a fifteen-foot statue of the King stands outside. "In my mind he is so large, bigger even than this," Uri Yoali, the owner, says. "Elvis is my life." Inside the inn, over seven hundred Elvis photos line the walls, and Elvis is on the Muzak system all the time.

Who knows how many home Elvis shrines there are worldwide? Certainly they must number in the tens of thousands throughout the United States, England, Europe, and beyond. Elvis icons and relics may occupy a corner of the family room, or fill an entire room, a bedroom, a rumpus room, a basement. Nothing remotely on the scale of this adoration has been accorded any mere secular hero in this, or perhaps any, century. There's clearly something quite pagan about them. One thinks of the altars to the household gods in Buddhist homes and those of ancient Rome, or of the gaudily paganistic syncretic Christianity of Filipino Catholicism and Santeria. It makes absolutely no difference to the users that many of the objects that make up these shrines are mass-produced or store-bought. The gestalt, the shrine as a whole, is an Eliadean space created for worship, a homemade, handmade, grass-roots effulgence of faith, an eruption of idolatry; religion brought straight into the home, not segregated in an official church structure, sanctioned by any canonists or homogenized by an elite esthetic.

Elvis Presley Enterprises is busily merchandising icons and relics with the kind of vigor that the medieval Vatican had in selling papal indulgences, splinters of the true cross, and the finger bones of martyred saints. That EPE meanwhile officially opposes the idolatry—is a Vatican in spite of itself—is ironic and perhaps reprehensible, but its opposition has had little effect. (A hundred years from now will an Elvist Luther launch his ninety-five theses on the interplanetary cybernet, denouncing the sale of E's icons and declaring Graceland the seat of the Anti-Elvis?)

In his book *The Majic Bus*, Douglas Brinkley writes about going, like everyone else, across the street with his students after they have visited Graceland, to the all-Elvis shopping mall. Brinkley is disturbed and a little depressed to see the same people who'd been crying sincere tears in the Meditation Garden moments before now haggling over the prices of the Elvis nail clippers, ballpoint pens, and license plate holders. Brinkley is troubled by this enjambment of the sacred and the aggressively profane.

But isn't this simply human nature? People of all faiths behave differently when they're in their place of worship and when they stop to buy bagels on the way home. Perhaps something larger was bothering Brinkley—the mercantile origins and marketing momentum of Elvism. In other words, the way Elvis is sold.

In its iconography, however, the cult of Elvis is already light-years ahead of the cult of Jesus, precisely because of Elvis' universal marketing. It took Christians (the Western European branch, anyway) in the neighborhood of thirteen hundred years to begin standardizing their image of their man-god into the universally recognized holy-card Jesus, the bearded, long-haired, soulful-eyed ectomorph in long white robes and sandals. Through endless commercial reproduction, E's imagery was already standardized and universally familiar years before it was apotheosized into iconography.

Complaints about Elvism's commercialism echo a common notion that America in general has become "more secular" and therefore "less religious" in the last half of the twentieth century. Like most common notions, this idea is based on unquestioned presumptions. First, it is presumed that America was somehow more religious in some earlier golden age, and second, that taking advantage of "secular" media to spread religious messages is a modern phenomenon.

Both presumptions are false, according to Cornell history professor R. Laurence Moore, the author of *Selling God*. Since very early in American history, Moore argues, churches have been centrally involved in the development of popular culture and mass media, sometimes adopting commercial techniques, but just as often innovating and inventing. "Religious leaders have as much claim to being seen as inventors of our popular cultural forms as anybody else," Moore says. "I say that without passing any judgment. I don't know how else religion could have operated."

The mass market for trashy paperback books, for instance, was created by the publishers of religious tracts, Moore argues. In the mid-1700s, evangelist George Whitefield could draw as many as eighty thousand people to his open-field revival meetings. His ability to mesmerize a crowd was admired by David Garrick, the great actor, and Ben Franklin alike. Descriptions of the frenzies he and other early evangelists could whip a crowd into make their revival meetings sound not unlike Elvis concerts. Successful nineteenth-century evangelists like Henry Ward Beecher (half-brother to Harriet Beecher Stowe) liberally borrowed theatrical techniques to keep their congregations entertained; mid-1800 training manuals for revival preachers read much like acting primers. Beecher was also adept at such "secular" pursuits as publicity and self-promotion and became a national celebrity. P. T. Barnum, unquestionably the nation's greatest publicity genius before the Colonel, borrowed astutely from p. r. techniques developed by Beecher and others.

By the end of the 1800s, Protestant leaders were rather comfortable with—and often championed—the notion of applying business know-how to doing God's work. They had little choice. "Religion is not after all saying 'Let's go out there and make a lot of money' in the same way that, say, the president of General Motors is," Moore explains. "They are, however, caught in the logic of expansion, of bureaucratization, routinization. They want to grow, they want to expand the market for the church, they have to pay all the workers. . . . To carry out the work of the church, to evangelize the world, requires enormous resources. It requires money. The Catholic Church never had any particular problem with that," he chuckles, "but Protestants worried about it."

In this century preachers were among the first to appreciate the potentials of radio, and later, tv. They were designing religious programming in radio's infancy, years before it had any commercial applications, and they started working with NBC to develop religious tv programming as early as the 1930s. Rex Humbard hit tv in 1952; Oral Roberts in 1955; Pat Robertson founded his own network, CBN, in 1960. Ben Armstrong, head of National Religious Broadcasters in the sixties, was a fan of Marshall McLuhan. He believed, Moore writes, that "understanding media was the key to proselytizing the world in the end times. Armstrong spotted a scriptural allusion to the appearance of satellite discs. They were prefigured in the angel mentioned in Revelation 14:6, 7. An angel 'weighing forty-seven hundred pounds, measuring eighteen feet in width, flying in geosynchronous orbit twenty-two thousand miles above the earth' appealed to the statistical bent in premillennial prophecy."

At what point does the selling of religion become too "crassly commercial"? Moore suggests it's a question of taste and class affiliation. Compared to the antics of some televangelists, the ministries of Bishop Fulton J. Sheen and Norman Vincent Peale were as sedate as corporate board meetings, their quiet sermons aimed at the educated middle class. Yet both built tv and publishing empires that were more profitable than those of Jimmy Swaggart or Oral Roberts. Did their greater profitability make them more crassly commercial?

Moore's argument could be extended to Elvism. Is Elvism's commercialism more crass than Jimmy Swaggart's? More crass than the 700 Club's, or Billy Graham's? More crass than the Catholic Church's aggressive marketing and sales of pope souvenirs and memorabilia?

■ ■ ■

Cowan's idolatrous portrait of Elvis at Graceland is not the only Elvis image that has attained a miraculous aura. In 1992, much in the way people have seen the image of Jesus appear on tacos, water towers, and garage floors, Eddie Fadal saw Elvis' image mysteriously appear—or rather disappear—on a wall in his basement in Waco, Texas.

A longtime friend of E's, Fadal maintained arguably the best private collection of Elvisiana anywhere until his death in 1994, including many items that had been given to him by Elvis himself. In 1992 *Elvis International Forum* ran a report by Caitlyn Stanley called "Elvis Vanishes!":

> A priceless photograph of Elvis has all but vanished into thin air. Only fragments of the face of the King remain, clinging hauntingly to a wall in Waco, Texas. You can still see the left eye, the nose and the mouth. . . .
>
> The original photograph was given to Eddie Fadal by Elvis in 1958. Strangely, it was the only object that attracted an army of termites. Everything else in the jam-packed room—the largest known Elvis collection, outside

Graceland—is untouched. Fadal questions, "Why would termites pick that photo—the only one Elvis ever gave to me personally? . . . Why would the insects ignore all these hundreds and hundreds of other pictures? Why didn't they eat on something else? And why was Elvis' face left on my wall like this? At first I thought maybe the picture had gotten wet—and had gotten damaged that way. But when I tried to get it down from the wall, the frame came off. The remains of the photo—this partial face of Elvis—just stuck to the wall."

The article goes on to report that Fadal recounted a young woman who'd visited Fadal's collection a short time before

"mentioned that she was having a strong feeling of Elvis' presence in here—in this room. Then, a few seconds later, every picture on that shelf went over—just like dominoes! There was no wind, no one was near them, and nothing shook the room. They just dumped over!" Fadal says that he usually scoffs at those reports of Elvis' face appearing in the clouds, or showing up on a screen door—but this has him baffled. He didn't want to do anything to publicize it at first. Then after everyone who came to see it begged him to put it out for the public—and for Elvis' fans—he decided to go ahead.

"One time years ago Elvis put up his open hand toward me, and said, 'Eddie Fadal is one of my five best friends in the world.' To me he was more like a son. . . . Why would the termites go to this very photograph? So many people have spoken to me about experiencing a 'presence' in this room. Just look at that image on the wall. Is there some sort of message in this?"

. . .

One of the most important symbols of Elvism is the "Taking Care of Business—In A Flash" symbol. E coined this motto to signify the level of obedience and performance he expected from his boys. Designed by E himself, the symbol shows the acronym atop a lightning bolt:

A Hollywood jeweler created an original thirteen TCB pendants in solid gold: one for E and the rest for twelve chosen apostles. Today they're highly prized relics sought after by movie stars and millionaire country singers. Inexpensive reproductions are sold as pendants, brooches, or pins; there are also TCB decals and bumper stickers. The symbol is sold all over Memphis and at Elvist gift shops and fans' swap meets everywhere. If not yet as ubiquitous as the Christians' cross or fish symbol, it is one of the simplest and most pervasive of Elvist identifiers.

On display during Tribute Week '94 in a case in a motel lobby near Graceland was the original "TCB Oath," a rare holographic artifact, scrawled in E's own hand on the corner of an envelope during a flight from L. A. to Memphis in 1971. It could become as important a document to Elvism as a fragment of the Dead Sea Scrolls. It reads:

> More self-respect, more respect for fellow man.
> Respect for fellow students and instructors.
> Respect for all styles and techniques.
> Body conditioning, mental conditioning, meditation for
> calming and stilling of the mind and body.
> Sharpen your skills, increase mental awareness for all those
> who might choose a new outlook and personal philosophy.
> Freedom from constipation.

TCB TECHNIQUE
All techniques into one

Elvis Presley, 8th [degree black belt]
Applying all techniques into one.

For the rest of the seventies, E was in the habit of administering this oath to his entourage, knighting them with a gold TCB pendant. The Oath is clearly a confluence of several of the King's major preoccupations: karate, spiritualism, and the blocked bowels that would increasingly trouble him, literally up until the moment of his death. "All techniques into one" is a trope of singular compression, summing up E's long pursuit of a New Ageish synthesis of beliefs and practices into a coherent lifestyle.

As every religion needs its one universally recognized sign, its cross, star-and-crescent, or star of David, Elvists are well on their way to adopting the TCB as theirs. One pictures two future Elvist pilgrims, strangers to each other, meeting on a dark corner of Beale Street or Lamar or Elvis Presley Boulevard:

"TCB, mama."

"All techniques into one."

With smiles of kinship, they embrace.

■ ■ ■

Artists and fiction writers, especially in the science fiction and fantasy genres, have always responded to the ineffable lure of Elvis iconography. Although their interpretation of it has typically been ironic and often scornfully elitist, arty types were among the first to accept the inevitability of the Elvist religion. Art-world Elvism has been well documented by the art world itself, and it continues to grow every year.

In 1995 "Dr." Karl Edwards of Hoboken and "Reverend" Mort Farndu of Denver announced the founding of the First

Presleyterian Church of Elvis the Divine. It was essentially a p. r. campaign to find a publisher for their manuscript "The Gospel According to Elvis," although for a $9.95 donation one would receive an official church membership card.

The Presleyterian creed wittily tapped into all the usual jokes about Elvis. "We sing his praises and praise his singing, for truly Elvis is our rock *and* our roll," Edwards proclaimed. The church listed thirty-one sacred items, virtually all of them Elvis' favorite foods, and exhorted members to overindulge, eating "six squares a day. . . with frequent snacks in between." Use of "many wondrous substances as prescribed by your physician" was approved. Presleyterians were expected to pray to Las Vegas once a day and make the pilgrimage to Graceland once in their lives.

The Memphis Mafia seemed to play a small role in the Presleyterian gospels, but Colonel Parker was a major figure— "the Colonel of Truth," who went before the King, proclaiming his divinity and making straight the way in those wicked dens of iniquity known as RCA and Hollywood. On a heavier note, Edwards warned, "It's now or never—the Second Comeback is nigh." Presleyterian scripture predicts that this will be between December 25, 1999, and January 8, 2000. On that blessed day, according to Reverend Farndu, Elvis "will appear on every tv screen, every movie screen, and every computer screen. All the phones in the world will start ringing at once," and it will be Elvis on every line, calling his faithful to join him in "that great Graceland in the sky," where he will "reach out his arms, give us all a big hug and say 'Let's eat.'" Everybody will get a pink Cadillac, and "we will all frolic with the King" in a heavenly Jungle Room.

Since 1987 some artists in Portland, Oregon, have maintained an Elvis icon boutique, the 24-Hour Church of Elvis. It sells Church of Elvis t-shirts, bumper stickers, refrigerator magnets, Christmas cards, and a cloth "Shroud of Elvis." At MIT there's an Elvis shrine complete with icons, an altar, and candles; in 1994, it earned its own home page on the World Wide Web. An unrelated Elvis home page emanating from the University of North Carolina ran afoul of Elvis Presley Enterprises in 1994, and EPE shut down for a while the "virtual Graceland tour" that was offered.

Appearing on the Internet in 1995 was the "Lesser Elvis Banishing Ritual of the Sequined Pentagram," a ritual for banishing "Elvis-negative influences" that its author claimed was "dictated to me whilst scrying into the black, shiny part of an Elvis record." Facing Graceland, you begin the ritual:

1: Visualize the infinitely bright light of a Las Vegas spotlight descending upon you.
2: Draw this Holy Light into your head, intoning: LOVE ME
3: Point downward, hand over . . . personal privates . . ., intoning: TENDER
4: Point to right shoulder. LOVE ME
5: Point to left shoulder. TRUE

This is the Holy Cross of Elvis. Conclude by saying: "Uh-huh."

You continue the visualizations, first seeing "Elvis as a baby, containing his True Elvis Potential. This is the Elvis of Air. Say: ELVIS, thou who were born a King in Lowly Surroundings. Fulfill your potential. Be present with me today." Next you envision "the young man Elvis, on the brink of Stardom. This is the Elvis of Water. Say: ELVIS, thou who art about to realize your Kingliness among men. Fulfill that Potential. Be with me today." Next, Elvis "in the prime of his career, when he was making movies and the like. He thrusts his pelvis suggestively. This is the Elvis of Fire. Say: ELVIS, thou who art leading us to Light. Be with me today." And finally, the Las Vegas Elvis, "slightly pudgy. This is the Elvis of Earth. Say: ELVIS, thou who didst die on the pot of an over-dose. Be with me today."

The ritual is complete. "May the Holy Light of Las Vegas Shine within you. Love is the Law. Love under Rock & Roll."

In 1994 Memphis curator Wendy McDaris created a trav-eling exhibition, "Elvis + Marilyn: 2 × Immortal," with iconog-raphy by 107 artists, including Elvis and Marilyn altars, crucified jumpsuits, and artists' documentation of Graceland pilgrimages. It prompted a long article in the Sunday edition of the *New York Times* headlined "A Pair of Saints Who Refuse to Stay Dead," in which art critic Vicki Goldberg wrote: "Elvis! He died for our sins; he died *from* our sins—addictions, pre-scriptions, success, excess, bad taste. He lives on in parking lots and shopping malls, blessing his aging devotees with visions of Himself between pickup trucks and plastic curlers and inchoate longings. The King must die but still he lives . . . right here in mass-reproduction heaven."

In his sci-fi novel *Elvyssey,* Jack Womack constructs a fully institutionalized Church of Elvis that has not only survived but become the official state religion of his alternate-reality future. In a short story called "The Sacred Treasures of Graceland: Excerpts from the Sanctioned Museum Catalogue" (antholo-gized in the all-Elvis short story collection *The King Is Dead*), Nancy A. Collins—a New York writer who worked at Grace-land in 1981—envisions Elvist icons of the twenty-first cen-tury. She imagines a day-glo Elvis Last Supper, yet another Velvet Elvis Shroud, and a painting of Gladys as the Virgin Mother being approached by the Holy Ghost in the form of the American eagle, announcing the imminent birth of the King. Collins pictures an engraving from A.D. 2000, *The King Approached by the Lesser Elvii,* illustrating a scene from "the Tupelo Apocrypha": "Here we see the lean, swaggering King—armed with his dimestore guitar—walking along a rocky valley floor. From the shadows of the rocks and crags emerge the Lesser Elvii—pale, flawed copies of the original, such as Fabian, Frankie Avalon, and Ricky Nelson—reaching out blindly in the direction of the divine light emanating from his self."

These imaginary icons, as Collins notes, are not far different from the actual ones we see around us every day. The line dividing other artistic and fictional extrapolations from actual Elvism is likewise far from clear. How different is the 24-Hour Church of Elvis' Christmas card from the one featuring Cowan's praying Elvis? Only the thinnest veneer of self-conscious irony distinguishes MIT's homage to Elvis from sincere shrines maintained by Elvis' fans. With even the *Wall Street Journal* and the *New York Times* art critics having begun to catch on, you need some pretty fine instruments to measure the gap between the irony and the reality.

FROM

CULT TO

RELIGION

If you really believe in Elvis, if you are a good person,
if you follow God, Elvis can hear you.
Judy Carroll

I F ELVISTS ARE chary about being called a religion, they
utterly deplore the notion that they're an "Elvis cult." Since
the seventies the term "cult" has come to be used in an
almost exclusively pejorative way. A cult is the Manson
Family, the People's Temple, Satanism, and the Order of the
Solar Temple. To many, cults represent an international conspiracy that by the late 1970s had spawned an entire cult
menace industry, which in turn spawned dozens of best-
selling books and thousands of hours of talk shows. Anti-
cultists developed commando squads to infiltrate cult centers,
kidnap, and then "deprogram" cult members against their will,
often in flagrant disregard for a number of their constitutional
rights. Responding to criticisms that their tactics were as dra-
conian, and possibly as psychologically damaging, as those of
the cult leaders they opposed, the deprogrammers later soft-
ened their image from that of quasi SWAT teams to kindly
quasi social workers who offered "exit counseling" to escaped
cultists. Their earlier militaristic methods set a precedent of

sorts for the 1993 fiasco of the federal government's deadly siege on David Koresh's Branch Davidian "cult menace" in Waco, Texas, the medieval echoes of which (the siege warfare, the torching of the heretics) seemed largely to escape media comment—at least until the tragic repercussions in Oklahoma City two years later prompted a reevaluation.

Christians today sometimes forget that their own religion began as a "cult menace." A charismatic leader, Jesus attracted a small group of devoted fans with his dangerous ideas and, by all reports, his working of miracles. When he was killed for his ideas, his followers were convinced that he would be resurrected, returning to them one day soon as their messiah. They fanned out and worked to convert nonbelievers.

In David Chidester's *Salvation and Suicide,* published in 1988, an attempt is made to balance the hype about Jim Jones with a little historical perspective. Chidester notes, "Alternative, marginal, or new religious movements in America have characteristically registered in the mainstream popular imagination as fundamentally other. They stand on the cognitive periphery of the dominant stream of American society, on the margin of the central religiopolitical order within American civil space, and they form something of a boundary definition for what may count as legitimate involvement in the central, common, and shared commitments of a mainstream worldview." Religious cultists are always relegated to one of two categories, Chidester writes; they must be either criminal or crazy. Extreme cases like Jim Jones and David Koresh are instantly assumed to have been both.

In 1981 religious historians David Bromley and Anson Shupe pointed out in their book *Strange Gods* that social scholars use the term "cult" nonjudgmentally, simply as a descriptor for "an organized set of beliefs and rituals surrounding some object of worship. Thus within modern Roman Catholicism there exists a cult of the Virgin Mary...just as in ancient Egypt certain gods, such as Isis and Osiris, were singled out for particular adoration. Outside of religion, similar cultlike followings surround Elvis Presley, the Beatles, and the television series *Star Trek*."

They furthermore noted that while most cults are short-lived, "a cult is the starting point of every religion. Its organization is extremely simple. There is no bureaucracy or priesthood. In fact, there is barely any structure at all except for the single charismatic leader and his or her small band of devoted followers. Jesus and his twelve disciples offer a classic example of a cult. Nor are there scriptures, not only because the cult rejects all or part of society's dominant religious traditions but also because it is simultaneously engaged in the act of creating its own traditions out of which later generations will record 'gospel' truths."

Cult activity did not suddenly appear in America in the 1970s. Since the English first began to settle here in the 1600s, this country has been home—most often unwillingly—to an incredible diversity of religious sects and cults, both imported and indigenous. This is partly the result of America's systemic guarantee of religious freedom, although this right may be more conceptual than it is put to practice.

Religious diversity in this country was the result of the American colonies, somewhat like those in Australia, having been the dumping ground for all sorts of religious dissidents, freethinkers, crackpots, and cranks of whom their home countries were just as happy to be rid. Puritanism came to define mainstream American religion and morals largely through numerical dominance in the early years, and the consequent ability to impose its own intolerance.

Historically, nearly every new belief system that has appeared in this country has come into conflict with this Protestant status quo. Many of these belief systems vanished, either perishing from active suppression or simply withering away for lack of followers. Groups that survived usually had to fight for their right to worship. Of those that did survive, several grew to become major American institutions. In other words, many of America's current mainstream religions started out as cults that were at least as bizarre as a People's Temple or Branch Davidians, and that were often just as feared and hated. American religious history is a parade of examples.

The early Society of Friends, nicknamed the Quakers for their fits of ecstatic worship, were founded in England by George Fox in the mid-1600s. The earliest Quaker missionaries in the New England colonies were everywhere harassed, fined, imprisoned, and deported. Four were put to death before Charles II intervened. By the 1680s the Quakers had survived and grown to be the fifth largest congregation in the colonies; starting around 1700 their missionary zeal cooled and they developed the quietly pacifist, progressivist character they're known for today.

The Anabaptists originated in Munich as a revolutionary political-millenarian sect who took over and ruled that town for three years in the 1530s. By the early 1600s they had quieted down and won respect from Rotterdam to Switzerland for their peaceful ways; they survive in the United States today as the thoroughly pacifistic Mennonites.

Like the Quakers, the Shakers got their nickname from their habit of becoming seized with a mighty trembling, and violent agitations of the body during their services of worship. Founder Ann Lee (1736-1784), the wife of a Manchester blacksmith, received visions that sex was the root of all evil and that Christ's Second Coming was at hand. Toward the end of her life, she and her followers became convinced that she herself was the Second Coming, in female form, and she was said to work miracles. In this sense, millennialist scholar Ted Daniels reasons, the Shakers were the first "radical feminists" in America. Today the Shakers are remembered chiefly for their elegant, simple furniture and a handful of hymns that became classic American folk songs.

Some of America's earliest sects were not Christian, but pagan. In the 1620s a freethinker named Thomas Morton wandered away from the Puritan Plymouth colony to found a wilderness trading post—and, in effect, his own neopaganist religion, embracing Indians and disaffected colonists alike in a Dionysian spirit of drinking, dancing, and general merry-making. He called his settlement Merry Mount, and erected a giant maypole around which he and his pilgrim bacchantes danced to joyful songs of his own devising, with lyrics like:

Drink and be merry, merry, merry boyes,
Let all your delight be in Hymen's joyes
and Lasses in beaver coats [i. e., Indian girls] come away,
Ye shall be welcome to us night and day.

The Pilgrim Fathers, not surprisingly, were unamused with these scandalous antics. Morton boasted of himself, "Hee that played Proteus (with helpe of Priapus) put their noses out of joynt." No less a figure than Miles Standish (whom Morton derided as "Captain Shrimp") was sent to break up the fun and arrest Morton, who spent the next twenty years in and out of jail, exile, and misery.

Can faith in Elvis be any stranger than Mormons' faith in Joseph Smith's bizarre visions? Smith, a native of Palmyra, New York, went out to the woods, where he received personal visits from God the Father, Jesus, and the angel Moroni, who led him to golden tablets on which was written, in a "Reformed Egyptian" hieroglyphics that was instantly translated for him when he put on a pair of rose-colored spectacles, the Book of Mormon, which he published in 1830.

The Book of Mormon, said to be an ancient text, relates the story of two lost tribes of Israelites who'd come to America around the time of the Babylonian exile of the Jews—the Nephites (including Mormon and Moroni) and Lamanites (American Indians). According to Smith's tablets, America was in fact the biblical promised land. Christ himself had come to America after his death and resurrection to organize the tribes, but the Lamanites later rebelled and destroyed the Nephites.

The doctrinal lessons Smith received in his visions led him farther and farther away from conventional Protestantism—most scandalously, in the practices of polygamy and something akin to ancestor worship, which forms the basis of the Mormons' famed skills in tracing geneology. Harassed by neighbors and government, the Mormons fled farther and farther west into the wilderness. The Mormons fought bloody pitched battles with the U. S. Army, and Smith was murdered by an angry mob, before Brigham Young led the great trek to Utah, "Zion in the Wilderness." Despite facing some of the most concentrated opposition any religious group has encountered in this country, Mormonism achieved astonishing growth in its followers, wealth, and political power. In many ways it has become the most successful "cult menace" in American history and even retains much of its cultish secrecy and separatism.

On the surface the contemporary cult of snake handling bears little resemblance to Elvism. Snake handlers form an extremist offshoot of fundamentalist Christianity that originated in East Tennessee in the early 1900s. They call their belief Pentecostal Holiness "with signs following," from the Gospel of Mark 16:17-18, which declares: "And these signs shall follow them that believe. In my name they shall cast out devils; they shall speak with new tongues; they shall take up serpents; and if they drink any deadly thing, it shall not hurt them; they shall lay hands on the sick and they shall recover."

Accordingly, they "take up" venomous snakes (rattlers, water moccasins, copperheads, and so on) as part of their services. They also drink strychnine (sometimes cut with Kool-

Aid) and handle fire. Many are maimed or killed in the process, but others survive dozens of bites over the years.

As is true of Elvism, snake handling is easily condemned as a wacky pursuit of ignorant poor white trash. Numbering no more than a few thousand practitioners scattered in tiny congregations of fifty members or less, they have been persecuted by media and prosecuted by law enforcement throughout the twentieth century.

Coming to the United States via Cuba, Santeria also met with a hostile and prejudiced reception. Practiced by slaves from the West African Yoruban culture, Santeria had always been looked down on, if not actively repressed, by the Catholic ruling classes in Cuba as well. To survive, Santeria enthusiastically borrowed many Catholic trappings—there are Santeria "masses," and many of the orishas, Santeria's gods, are closely identified with Catholic saints. Shango, the Santeria god-king who traditionally wears red, became Saint Barbara, the patron saint of soldiers, who is traditionally depicted wearing a crown and a red cloak. Babalu Aye, the orisha who rules over smallpox, was associated with the leper Lazarus. Obatala wears the outer appearance of the Catholics' Our Lady of Mercy, Oshun takes on the guise of Our Lady of Charity, and so on.

Santeria scholar Raul Canizares explains that this syncretism is not an "unconscious, uncritical adoption of the dominant culture's religious beliefs," but a clever dissimulation, a screen of accepted images and icons behind which Afro-Cubans could practice their beliefs without being hassled. It's not very different, he contends, from the way pagans in early medieval Europe were able to keep their gods and practices alive by disguising them as Catholic saints and rites. Thus St. Bridget was the Catholicized version of a Celtic goddess, the cult of the Virgin had aspects of earlier cults of Diana, and the celebration of Christmas has its origins in the Yule festival of pagan Germans. Ismaili Muslims practiced similar deceptions to hide their true beliefs from the more powerful Sunni.

"From a santero's perspective," Canizares writes in his book *Walking with the Night*, "it is not wrong to celebrate a feast to the orishas on Saturday night and go to mass Sunday morning. Many santeros have developed a genuine affection for Catholic saints and enjoy mass for the same reasons other Catholics do. . . . However, knowledgeable santeros are perfectly aware of the differences between the orishas and the saints."

Elvism's syncretism, its many borrowings from and echoes of Christianity, is simply an unconscious reflection of the culture Elvists grew up and live in. Maybe it also provides the same sort of protective cover Santeria takes in its Catholic trappings. The mockery of outsiders who make Jesus-and-Elvis jokes is nothing like persecution, but would Elvism be more actively suppressed if its believers declared their faith in Elvis-the-god outright?

■ ■ ■

As the year 2000 approaches, a lot of modern cult activity has taken on a decidedly millenarian and apocalyptic flavor. Ted Daniels founded and edits *Millennial Prophecy Report,* a newsletter that tracks this apocalyptic trend. I spoke to him in early 1995, and he readily agreed that Elvism is a modern cult that, with its messianic strain, fits easily with other apocalyptic movements.

In fact, Daniels tells me, the wide variety of apocalyptic notions brewing in America at the end of the millennium is much broader than many people seem to understand, and it includes many secular as well as religious expressions. "America is especially prone to this," he says. "We're founded on a millennialist ideology. We've been steeped in it ever since. It's been unexplicit and inarticulate, but it's been there all the way through. I mean, Columbus thought he was going to find the Lost Ten Tribes and bring them back to Israel to prepare for the Second Coming. The pilgrims came here to found the New Jerusalem, the city on the hill. It goes right down to James Watt—'Why save the forests for the next generation? That's not going to happen.'

"The entire New Age is a millennialist trend," he goes on. "And then you've got the secular millennialists. You've got the World Watch Institute talking exactly like a biblical prophet. 'We've got ten years, clean up your act or it's all over for us.' The same structure to the rhetoric, the same ideas. The ecology movement is a millennialist movement. No divine intervention, maybe, but it sure is."

Accelerated social change breeds end-of-the-world preoccupations, Daniels believes. "You get up to a certain level of change going on, which is what we're swept up in right now, and change spooks everybody. It's unpredictable. You don't know how it's all going to come out. You don't know how *you're* going to come out when it all shakes down. Are you going to be alive, are you going to have a job, or have any way to live at all? Situations like that, that's when people start looking for some certainty. And that's what religion is. Now, what's going on here is that your old standby religions are going down the tubes. So who do you turn to? You look to the innovators. That's who the prophets always are."

Daniels rejects any notion that apocalypse obsessions are limited to the lunatic fringe. He notes that Hal Lindsey's *Late Great Planet Earth* was *the* best-selling book of the 1970s. It's still in print and has sold over twenty-five million copies. He refers to the recent Gallup poll indicating that 40 percent of Americans believe that every word of the Bible is literal truth. "A hundred million people is a pretty big fringe. It's fringe in Wall Street, it's fringe in Washington, it's fringe in Hollywood, where the elite power centers are. But it ain't fringe anywhere else." As for the power elite, he says, "In fact, *they're* the fringe—but try to convince them of that."

One thing Elvists have in common with other millennial groups is the way the very nature of their beliefs makes them easy targets of mockery. Daniels cites the late Sister Phaedra, leader of a UFO group that predicted the day on which the alien space fleet was scheduled to land in Cleveland. "They notified the media, and everybody flocked to Cleveland to watch them be humiliated. The laughter carried on like crazy, and psychologists said, 'Well, they're going to go off and hide someplace—fold up their tent and vanish.'" In fact, after all the media attention, Sister Phaedra's group found themselves recruiting new members faster than ever.

Preacher Harold Camping pegged the Second Coming for September 1994. Rather than suffer embarrassment when September uneventfully came and went, he pointed to all the press he'd gotten and claimed it as a tremendous success for his ministry. The Unification Church in its early years easily assimilated every new setback, every new round of bad press; it served only to confirm their belief that the world was filled with evil. They found this confirmation "in any negative event," Daniels says. "Say somebody promised to come to a meeting and didn't show. It meant Satan was at work. And the harder Satan was working, the more threat they were to him."

Sociologist Peter Worsley has argued that the cults that survive and grow into full-fledged religious institutions are the ones that are successful at "converting chiliastic immediacy" into more vague, delayed gratifications. That is, they organize at first around a living leader or around the anticipation of an immediate, often apocalyptic, outcome. When the leader dies, or the apocalypse fails to arrive on schedule, the followers must redirect their expectations toward more distant goals, or the group falls apart. Thus, when the prophesied apocalypse did not arrive on schedule for either the Seventh Day Adventists or the Jehovah's Witnesses in the nineteenth century, they stopped expecting the Second Coming and threw their millenarian zeal into global missionary work instead.

Perhaps Sister Phaedra's and Harold Camping's followers will display similar determination and devotion. Perhaps Elvists will as well.

■ ■ ■

The last decades of the twentieth century are rife with examples of religious or spiritual movements that are, at best, distrusted by the mainstream. Pentecostal and charismatic movements are currently the fastest-growing wings of Christianity in America, and Christian fundamentalism is thriving as well. In Judaism, cultic messianic sects like Brooklyn's Lubavitchers are strong and growing. The great resurgence in fundamentalist Islam is a small but growing immigrant force in the United States, as are Santeria and related Yoruban-derived systems brought north by immigrants from the Caribbean and South America.

Under the generic rubric of New Age beliefs a panoply of systems continues to sprout. There are cult groups influenced by Hinduism and Japanese Buddhism. There are Wiccans, channelers, and other occultist groups; neopagans, "modern primitives," and other neotribal groups; Gaia/Goddess worshippers; several thriving cults like Sister Phaedra's, dedicated to UFO space aliens, and so on. And despite roughly a quarter-century of mainstream disfavor, flagship cults from the seventies like the Unitarian Church and the Church of Scientology continue to thrive.

Each of these presents an alternative to dominant religious practices, which is part of why they're distrusted and disliked. Historically, few alternative American beliefs have lived up to their reputations as powerful threats to civil order. Jim Jones was almost certainly mad; the Branch Davidians were certainly amassing an arsenal of heavy firearms; other cult leaders have certainly inflicted psychological, sexual, and financial abuse on their followers. Ultimately, however, even the maddest cults usually prove dangerous only to themselves, and many cults who were perceived to be mad or bad were feared only because they were *different*.

A lot of people seem to think that Elvis' faithful are also mad, yet the cult of Elvis doesn't conform to common notions of what cults are and how "cult madness" works. There's no tyrannical Jim Jones or David Koresh figure enforcing blind obedience, yanking the faithful away from their everyday lives, demanding sacrifice—sometimes the ultimate sacrifice—as proof of allegiance to him. There's only Elvis, who never made any demands at all on his fans, and those who have freely elected to be his faithful. Outsiders do not perceive the Elvis faith as threatening or dangerous to society; at worst, it strikes them as merely outlandish and pitiful. Although it is marginalized, much of it is mainstream—it is a religion based on love of Elvis Presley and rock 'n' roll. Outsiders don't fear it, they just laugh at it.

Who knows whether the People's Temple or Branch Davidians, had they survived their confrontations with the law and their own inner strife, might eventually have quieted down, become mainstream and as powerful as the Mormons?

Who knows what will become of the Elvis faith? The fact that outsiders can't take it seriously may turn out to be its strength and its shield. Elvis worship has elicited nothing like persecution—only bad press and derision. Taken more seriously, it might already have been destroyed. Maybe by the time Elvism is taken seriously it will have quietly grown too large and well established to be crushed like the Branch Davidians.

bibliography

Bennett, Gillian. *Traditions of Belief.* New York: Viking Penguin, 1987.

Birckhead, Jim. "'Bizarre Snake Handlers': Popular Media and a Southern Stereotype." In *Images of the South,* edited by Karl G. Heider. Athens: University of Georgia Press, 1993.

Brewer-Giorgio, Gail. *Is Elvis Alive?* New York: Tudor, 1988.

Brinkley, Douglas. *The Majic Bus.* San Diego: Harcourt Brace Jovanovich, 1993.

Bromley, David G., and Anson D. Shupe, Jr. *Strange Gods.* Boston: Beacon Press, 1981.

"Brother Randall," ed. *Snake Oil,* 1993–94, 1–3.

Brown, Patricia Leigh. "A Decade After Elvis: Faithful at the Shrine." *New York Times,* August 13, 1987.

———. "Candles in the Dark: 2 Sides of Elvis." *New York Times,* August 16, 1987.

Burk, Bill E., and Connie Lauridsen Burk, eds. *Elvis World,* 1994, 30–32.

Burton, Sir Richard F. *Personal Narrative of a Pilgrimage to Al-Madinah and Meccah.* Mineola, N. Y.: Dover, 1964.

Butler, Brenda Arlene. *Are You Hungry Tonight?* New York: Gramercy Books, 1992.

Campbell, Joseph. *The Masks of God.* New York: Viking Penguin, 1964.

———, with Bill Moyers. *The Power of Myth.* New York: Doubleday, 1988.

Canizares, Raul. *Walking with the Night.* Shippensburg, Pa.: Destiny Image, 1993.

Chidester, David. *Salvation and Suicide.* Bloomington: Indiana University Press, 1988.

Choron, Sandra, and Bob Oskam. *Elvis: The Last Word.* New York: Citadel, 1991.

Connell, Janice T. *The Visions of the Children.* New York: St. Martin's Press, 1992.

Corrigan, Robert W., ed. *Euripides.* New York: Dell, 1965.

Dawidoff, Nicholas. "No Sex. No Drugs. But Rock 'N' Roll (Kind Of)." *New York Times,* February 5, 1995.

De Vries, Jan. *Perspectives in the History of Religions.* Berkeley: University of California Press, 1977.

Dundy, Elaine. *Elvis and Gladys.* New York: Macmillan, 1985.

Eicher, Peter. *The Elvis Sightings.* New York: Avon, 1993.

Elliott, Lawrence. "Where Elvis Lives." *Reader's Digest,* August 1993.

Elvis Presley's Graceland: The Official Guidebook. Memphis: Elvis Presley Enterprises, 1993.

Farren, Mick. *The Hitchhiker's Guide to Elvis.* London: Collector's Guide, 1994.

Fearheiley, Don. *Angels Among Us.* New York: Avon, 1993.

Festinger, Leon, Henry W. Riecken, and Stanley Schachter. *When Prophecy Fails.* Minneapolis: University of Minnesota Press, 1956.

Geller, Larry, and Joel Spector with Patricia Romanowski. *"If I Can Dream": Elvis' Own Story.* New York: Simon and Schuster, 1989.

Gesch, Patrick F. *Initiative and Initiation.* Berlin: Anthropos-Institut, 1985.

Gibbs, Nancy. "Angels Among Us." *Time,* December 27, 1993.

Goldberg, Vicki. "A Pair of Saints Who Refuse to Stay Dead." *New York Times,* December 18, 1994.

Goldman, Albert. *Elvis.* New York: McGraw-Hill. 1981.

Greenberg, Allen H. *Secret Cipher of the UFOnauts.* Avondale Estates, Ga.: Illuminet, 1994.

Gregory, Neal, and Janice Gregory. *When Elvis Died.* New York: Pharos, 1992.

Guralnick, Peter. *Last Train to Memphis.* Boston: Little, Brown, 1994.

Hampton, Howard. "Elvis Dorado: The True Romance of *Viva Las Vegas*." *Film Comment,* July–August 1994.

Harris, Marvin. *Cannibals and Kings.* New York: Random House, 1977.

Harrison, Ted. *Elvis People.* New York: Fount, 1992.

Hazen, Cindy, and Mike Freeman. *The Best of Elvis.* New York: Pinnacle Books, 1994.

Hoggart, Simon. "Elvis of Nazareth." *The Economist,* July 1992.

Hudson, Winthrop S. *Religion in America.* New York: Charles Scribner's Sons, 1981.

I Am Elvis. New York: Pocket Books, 1991.

Keith, Jim, ed. *Secret and Suppressed: Banned Ideas and Hidden History,* Portland, Ore.: Feral House, 1993.

Knipfel, Jim. "The King's Asshole Speaks." Unpublished essay.

Lambert, Royston. *Beloved and God: The Story of Hadrian and Antinous.* New York: Viking Penguin, 1984.

Lamm, Darwin, ed. *Elvis International Forum,* 1988–94, 1–7.

Marcus, Greil. *Dead Elvis.* New York: Doubleday, 1992.

Moody, Raymond A. *Elvis After Life.* Atlanta, Ga.: Peachtree, 1987.

Peers, Alexandra. "Elvis Relics Fetch Big Bids at Vegas Sale." *Wall Street Journal,* June 20, 1994.

Pierce, Stephanie G. *Strange Mystery at the 24 Hour Church of Elvis.* Seattle: Where's the Art!!, 1994.

Presley, Priscilla, with Sandra Harmon. *Elvis and Me.* New York: G. P. Putnam's Sons, 1985.

Price, Hope. *Angels.* New York: Avon, 1994.

Price, Simon. "From Noble Funerals to Divine Cult: The Consecration of Roman Emperors." In *Rituals of Royalty,* edited by David Cannadine and Simon Price. New York: Cambridge University Press, 1987.

Quain, Kevin, ed. *The Elvis Reader.* New York: St. Martin's Press, 1992.

Reid, Jim. *Fond Memories of Elvis.* Self-published, 1991.

Robertson, John. *The Complete Guide to the Music of Elvis Presley.* London: Omnibus Press, 1994.

Rovin, Jeff. *The World According to Elvis.* New York: HarperCollins, 1992.

Sakolsky, Ron, and James Koehn-line, eds. *Gone to Croatan.* Brooklyn: Autonomedia, 1994.

Sammon, Paul M., ed. *The King Is Dead: Tales of Elvis Postmortem.* New York: Bantam Doubleday Dell, 1994.

Sennett, Richard. *Flesh and Stone.* New York: W. W. Norton, 1994.

Stern, Jane, and Michael Stern. *Elvis World.* New York: Alfred A. Knopf, 1987.

———. *Encyclopedia of Pop Culture.* New York: HarperCollins, 1992.

Threadwell, David. "King Elvis Still Reigns in Southern Lore." *Los Angeles Times,* August 17, 1987.

Umphred, Neal. "Elvis + Girls + Songs! Who Could Ask For More?" *Goldmine,* January 21, 1994.

———. "Elvis's Golden (And Not So Golden) Records." *Goldmine,* January 21, 1994.

Veyne, Paul, ed. *A History of Private Life.* Vol. 1, *From Pagan Rome to Byzantium.* Cambridge, Mass.: Belknap/Harvard University Press, 1987.

Washington, Peter. *Madame Blavatsky's Baboon.* New York: Schocken, 1995.

West, Red, Sonny West, and Dave Hebler. *Elvis: What Happened?* New York: Ballantine, 1977.

Wilson, Peter Lamborn. *Sacred Drift.* San Francisco: City Lights, 1993.

Womack, Jack. *Elvissey.* New York: Tor, 1993.

Worsley, Peter. *The Trumpet Shall Sound: A Study of "Cargo" Cults in Melanesia.* New York: Schocken Books, 1968.

Yourcenar, Marguerite. *Memoirs of Hadrian.* New York: Farrar, Straus & Giroux, 1963.

In addition to printed matter, source materials include the following videos and films: *Aloha from Hawaii; Blue Hawaii; Elvis: The Great Performances; Elvis on Tour; Elvis: That's The Way It Is; This Is Elvis; Elvis Stories; Elvis: The Early Years; Legends; Elvis and the Beauty Queen; Mondo Elvis; Mondo Cane; Viva Las Vegas; The Singer Special; Jailhouse Rock; Love Me Tender; Fun in Acapulco; Clambake; G. I. Blues;* and *Dancing Outlaw.*